Knowing Noah

Knowing Noah

The adventures of a Mouse who could read

DOUGLAS FLOEN

ILLUSTRATION
GLORIA KOYOUNIAN

authorHOUSE®

AuthorHouse™
1663 Liberty Drive
Bloomington, IN 47403
www.authorhouse.com
Phone: 1-800-839-8640

Published by AuthorHouse   07/19/2012

ISBN: 978-1-4772-4506-4 (sc)
ISBN: 978-1-4772-4505-7 (e)

Library of Congress Control Number: 2012912714

CHAPTER ONE

The Storm

I T ALL BEGAN WITH a blinding storm. Wind, thunder and pouring rain such as Wild Wold Farm had never seen. All the animals in the red and white barn were nervous and upset whenever lightning flashed and thunder shook the building.

In one of the stalls at the far side of the barn was a brick wall, and at the bottom of this wall a large crack had appeared many years ago when the barn was new and had begun to settle into its foundation.

This crack went past the brick and deep into the cement beneath. And it was in this crack that the mouse family lived. Grandpa Ezekiel, his wife and five, lively, baby mice all lived snug and secure, warm and dry until the night of the storm.

There had always been storms, it is part of nature's way, but this storm was more fierce and violent than anyone could remember.

Bolts of lightning crackled, crashes of thunder boomed and howling wind whipped the trees until they almost bent double. Down in buckets came the rain and, as it descended, Sparkling Stream, which usually ran so slowly and quietly through the farm meadows, began to rise and turn into a mighty foaming torrent. This swirling ocean of water rose over its banks and flooded the drowsy ferns and shady cool plants that lined the rocks alongside it. The stream began to spread in waves across the farm and over the doorsteps of the farm buildings. In the barn, the nervous large animals felt the cold water creep up and swirl about their legs. The ducks and geese loved this, but even they found it hard to swim against the insistent tide of water. The chickens just flew to higher perches, as did Snoad, the barn cat, who hates water passionately.

For our mouse family, it was a different story. As the first inquisitive fingers of water entered the cozy straw and feather nest deep in the foundation, Grandpa Ezekiel knew he must act and act quickly to save his family. He ordered the five mewling babies onto his back to cling tightly, as they had never clung before. As the water rushed into the warm nest, Grandpa started upward, pushing and struggling against the downward flow. Calling behind him for the mother mouse to grab onto his tail, he slowly alternated swimming and climbing and managed to make his way up and out of the dark wet tunnel and into the main part of the barn itself. Here all was chaos, as each barn animal gave forth with calls of distress and fear. Grandpa Ezekiel treaded water while he decided what to do next but being very quick witted, he noticed a wooden shingle floating nearby, freed from a pile of shingles that Farmer Boaz was using to re-roof the barn. As quick as a wink, Grandpa swam to the floating shingle, climbed awkwardly onto it and as he did so, the weight of the five babies and his wife who had clung onto his tails was too much, and the shingle flipped over, sending all the mice splashing into the murky water. Grandpa tried again to climb onto the shingle and this time he was successful, and why? Because he now only had one baby on his back. Through the dim light cast by a lantern nailed high on a post he could see the rest of his family struggling and panic-stricken, floating further and further away from him. Their tiny cries for help grew fainter, as the shingle was caught up in a current that was taking all floating objects, including the cheerful ducks out through the open barn door and into the raging storm. Grandpa clung to the bobbing shingle that twisted and turned in the boiling stream; now up, now down and around, it floated with sky, wind and pouring rain all becoming one frightening world of menace. Grandpa had no time to mourn his losses, but concentrated on keeping the one remaining baby safe beneath his belly, as he hung on to the uncontrollable fragment of wood.

There they stayed, floating along the rapid current, further and further away from the life they knew.

As dawn came and the storm passed over, the new day revealed a sad sight of drowned crops and soaked and sodden pastures. As the flood receded, farm objects appeared scattered about haphazardly. Shingles, straw, hose, rakes; anything that could float would be left, as though a giant hand had picked them up and thrown them out to land where they may.

The ducks and geese welcomed the dawn with their usual clamour, but everywhere else, there was an eerie silence. Farmer Boaz and his wife stood on their porch steps surveying the disaster with tears in their eyes. They knew that, with hard work, everything would be put right, but now, with the devastation before them, they felt helpless. Everywhere they looked, their once orderly farm was gone. With a look of determination, they set forth to begin the task of cleaning up.

And Grandpa Ezekiel? What of him and the remaining baby? Far away down the path of the now gently running Sparkling Stream, the shingle had snagged onto a wooden gate and had remained there, settling into the ground when the water receded. Grandpa sheltered the shivering baby and waited until the morning had dried off their soaked fur, before they crept into the bushes. They remained there all day, not knowing where to go or what to do next. Grandpa was able to find some grass seeds in a nearby bush, but this was all they had to eat. As night fell, Grandpa decided that they must make a move. With the tiny baby hanging onto his back for dear life, Grandpa ventured out. As he moved along, always on guard for owls, he wept for his lost family and became even more determined to save this tiny scrap clinging so trustingly to his back. Up a slight rise of land, Grandpa climbed and when he reached the top, he made out a solitary building standing alone in a darkening grove of pine trees. They made toward the building, up the steps and through a small crack between the front doors. Inside he was reassured by the quietness; nothing moved and a sense of peace radiated from the front where, on an altar, candles gave a comforting warm glow. Grandpa had found a church in the woods and here, he was to make his new home. Making sure that his one remaining baby was secure in a hidden corner filled with discarded papers, he crept out into the main part of the building and down the centre aisle. On either side of him arose gigantic wooden pews and he looked up in awe, as he made his way to the altar. He climbed quickly up, his little black eyes taking everything in, his whiskers twitching to pick up the smell of danger or food. Food! He smelled a lovely aroma and, after a short search, found a plate piled with thin bread wafers. He quickly satisfied his own hunger and, in the manner of mice everywhere, packed his cheeks to take back to the remaining baby. Full of food and settled comfortably in a nest of old papers, the two slept for a long time. They needed to repair the energy and restore the spirits that they had lost during the terrible events of the previous night.

The move to the church was a very lucky one, as people only used it once a week on Sunday morning. During the week, it was empty and silent, just perfect for two refugee mice. Grandpa explored and found that the ideal spot for a permanent nest was between the covers of a book, one of a pile in an unused cupboard. The book had very attractive gold edging to the leaves which were tissue thin and thus easy to chew. Little did he know that he was nesting in a Bible, and little did he know that a magical event was taking place. The baby mouse, in order to help, was busily chewing out a hollow for a nest in the book's leaves. As he chewed, he was unconsciously absorbing the language that they contained. The little mouse surprised Grandpa with his new-found ability one day, when he began reading aloud from the books lying about. Grandpa was astounded and he realized that for some magical reason, the baby had a gift that would, and could, set him apart from other mice. As he was a thoughtful mouse, Grandpa encouraged the little one to read and speak human language and so spent long hours perfecting his reading and speaking skills in that quiet candlelit place.

The young mouse was growing very quickly. He was handsome as mice go; he had thick sleek fur, a tawny brown color, and black little eyes, nose and tail.

Time passed and the little motherless mouse grew to rely upon himself for company as he was growing up without the companionship of other mice his own age and thus, he developed a solitary nature quite enjoying being by himself, or sitting with Grandpa and reading aloud in the candlelight.

One day, while reading to Grandpa, they came across a story about a terrible flood that had happened long ago and about a man named Noah, who had not only survived that flood but who had, by means of a giant boat, saved many animals and people.

"What a name for my boy," exclaimed Grandpa. "Noah will be his name and while he didn't save anyone he will be the one who saves our family name." From that time onward, the little mouse who survived the flood would be known as Noah.

Months went by, and while Grandpa and Noah led a contented life, something in his head made Grandpa restless and out of sorts. He knew deep inside that he wanted to return to his real home in Wild Wold Farm.

CHAPTER TWO

Going Home

ONE SUNNY, SPRING DAY, Grandpa said to Noah, "We must return to our true home, which I'm sure you scarcely remember." Noah did not remember it, but as he had developed a taste for reading about the adventures of others, he felt it was time to have some of his own, and so they set off, Grandpa lead the way, always wary of danger with Noah behind, eager to see, smell, and taste all that was new and exciting.

That evening, they arrived at the barn and Grandpa found that their nest, deep in the foundation crack was still there and by now had dried out. They settled in, after evicting a family of earwigs who had taken it over. The barn, for Noah to explore, was a huge place. The cement floor was divided into stalls for the horses and cows to feed and spend the night. There were large coops for the chickens and turkeys to return to after a day spent out of doors. Also on the barn floor were kept milk pails and the tools needed to keep the animals clean and dry.

It was the barn loft that Noah found of greatest interest when he began to find his way about. It was piled high with bales of hay and sweet smelling clover and it was clean, dry and safe.

The only animals ever to use it were mainly mice, roosting pigeons and the occasional owl or bat. Although the mice families nested in other parts of the barn, they all used the loft as a common area. Two very large triangular windows in the front provided a sweeping view of the whole farm. From here could be seen the course of Sparkling Stream and beyond the meadows, fields and outbuildings that made up Wild Wold Farm. At first, Noah tried very hard to fit into life with the other barn mice, but he found that games of Hide-and-Seed, Catch-the-Grains were boring. To Noah, the silliest of all, Catch-the-Berry-Ball consisted of tossing a ripe berry back and forth with no apparent purpose.

Noah was the odd one, and so he would go off on his own. The father and mother mice in the barn frowned upon Noah and his ways; they felt that it was a waste of time for mice to daydream. They wanted their children to play games and be educated in proper mouse behaviour such as: finding and storing grain and other edibles, camouflage, cat and owl behaviour, and fur grooming. They also had lessons in Nature Natter, a common language by which all animals could communicate.

Noah was stubborn and would have none of this; he had other things on his mind, lofty things he thought, things of his very powerful imagination. Something mystical had happened to Noah during that wild storm. A small bolt of lightning had hit him and changed the way he thought, giving him powers that no other mice had.

Grandpa Ezekiel found that returning home was harder than he first thought, mainly because of the problems involved with Noah. Settling back into his former home deep in the cracked barn foundation had not been hard. Some fresh feathers and down from generous ducks plus fragrant hay picked up from the barn floor made an inviting nest for the mice. Grandpa then went around the barn reacquainting himself with old friends, finding out who had lost family and what had become of everyone after the flood. One of the first things that concerned Grandpa was making sure that Noah should lead as normal a life as possible. In the loft, the mouse families had established a school run by a smart lady mouse called Madame Topal. Here, in this school, all young mice were expected to spend several hours each day learning mouse behaviour and mouse techniques. The lessons were valuable because they were designed to prepare young mice to survive in the sometimes harsh world of the barn. Grandpa made arrangements with Madame Topal to admit Noah to class. The first day a very reluctant Noah was brought to class by Grandpa.

"Here's my boy," he told a very stiff and upright Madame Topal. "He is bright and I want him to learn and fit right in." Madame Topal had taught generations of young mice and she had one simple rule; she was boss and there were no questions asked.

"Things will be just fine," replied Madame Topal. "Now sit up here in front of me, I like to keep a close eye on all newcomers." She treated Noah to a very sharp look and a very tiny smile. Reassured, Grandpa kissed Noah goodbye, much to Noah's embarrassment and to laughter behind paws of all the other young mice looking on.

Madame Topal called for attention, and went on with her lesson about the art of camouflage which was important to mice, as they needed to go unnoticed when appearing in open spaces. Noah was sitting up trying to concentrate when he felt his tail being pulled. He ignored this, but when later on, Madame Topal asked everyone to recite an oral drill, Noah stood up only to hear a cry and a thud! He turned around to look and he saw Madame Topal, flat on her back, struggling to untie her tail from his. Madame Topal had strolled behind him while talking and another mouse called Seymour had tied their tails together. When Noah rose to recite, he had jerked her tail from under her. Madame Topal was outraged as she tried to regain her dignity. Finally righting herself, she demanded to know who was responsible. All the little mice, laughing uncontrollably behind their paws, pointed to Noah. Madame Topal tore into Noah, not giving him a moment to defend himself as she ordered him home. From that day onward, Noah could do nothing right in her eyes, and that, together with the constant teasing of the other mice, made for a very unpleasant school experience.

Word had gotten around that Noah hung around with Snoad, the farm cat, and of all beasts, mouse hatred for cats is so deep that almost everyone who heard the story refused to believe it. "What self-respecting mouse would go near a cat and furthermore what self-respecting cat would allow it?" they said. Noah found himself more and more alone and, when the day dawned that the schoolroom finally found out that he thought he could read and understand human talk, Noah's life was not worth living. It happened on a day that Madame Topal was taking the class on a field trip to the farm rubbish dump. She was to teach them techniques in food scrap salvage and nest design using bits of discarded wool. As the young mice were having a short snack break, several of them had noticed that Noah had found, and was wearing, a tiny vest and a pair of discarded eyeglasses that he rescued from a broken doll. He was sitting on top of a pile of old newspapers and magazines.

"What are you up to?" inquired Seymour, who always took the lead in bullying. "Look everyone, nimwit Noah is pretending he can read." Everyone rushed over and circled around Noah who, angry, defensive and fed up with the constant teasing, lost his temper and shouted, "Yes I can read human language and I'm a lot smarter than you who can only speak Nature Natter." This revelation was met with stunned silence.

"Prove it," finally jeered Seymour, "prove it, nimwit!" and so an angry and confused Noah began to try to read aloud the first story he came to. He was so upset and nervous, tears streamed from his eyes and all he could do was stammer out weird sounding gabble. This made the young mice around him laugh so hard that Madame Topal, who had found a bit of red lace and was admiring herself in a broken mirror, rushed over and demanded to know what was going on.

"Nimwit Noah says he can read and talk human talk," sneered Seymour.

"Noah, get off that paper pile and come here to talk to me. What are you doing with that vest and those silly glasses? Are you trying to be like a human? Whatever put such silly and dangerous thoughts in your head? If you continue to behave in this unmouse-like way, I shall be forced to take drastic action." Just what this action was she didn't say, but Noah knew better than to argue.

"And that's not all," piped up Lucy, a close friend of Seymour's, "He plays with Snoad, the farm cat."

Madame Topal was so shocked at this new revelation that she wordlessly seized Noah's ear and marched him all the way back to the barn loft. There she punished him by having him hunt for, and to bring, old cobwebs to be made into cradles for baby mice. This was a nasty and difficult job, involving climbing high up inside the barn roof, tearing down old webs and carrying them to the school room. Noah sniffled and hung his head, knowing it would be pointless to try to explain himself to anyone. He laboured mightily with the silky cobwebs. As he did so, he thought about the day and began to understand for the first time that the natural world has rules, and sets very strict standards for all those living within it. Any change can upset the balance and thus, Noah grew up a little that day. He went home that night wrapped in cobwebs that Grandpa helped him get rid of. He curled up to sleep and dreamed of a time when everyone would understand him. He would do great things and all the mice would applaud him.

Grandpa watched his little mousekin with sad but understanding eyes. After all, it was he that had encouraged Noah to read in the first place and he felt responsible. There was nothing he could do, however, to improve Noah's social standing. That, he would have to deal with himself.

CHAPTER THREE

A Lesson Learned

NOAH WAS A VERY quiet, grave and respectful mouse but he did have his faults, one of which was his air of "knowingness". Because he could read he felt rather superior to other mice and never hesitated to show off his knowledge. Other mouse families, of which there were many, as in any barn, resented this. Several of whom were Noah's age decided one day that Noah should be taught a lesson. They planned to play a rather nasty trick on him. One of the mice children was named Seymour. As in any group there is a bully, and this one was Seymour. A rather large gray mouse, Seymour was of course tops at all games. He enjoyed his reputation and liked to swagger about with a group of his friends looking for ways to show himself off. He and his friends surrounded Noah one day as he was sitting enjoying the view from the window of the barn loft.

"You think you're so smart, never learning any of our lessons on mouse behaviour, always sitting by yourself pretending you know everything. I'll bet you don't know where the best earthworms on the farm are." Noah ignored this but his whiskers did twitch a little bit as, if there is one thing Noah loved, it was fat, juicy earthworms.

Seymour's friends all poked each other giggling and another one, Sally, said, "We know a place that is crawling with earthworms and they're just as easy to catch as that." With that she clapped her two front paws together quickly.

Now everyone was snickering, crowding around Noah, shoving and pushing him. "C'mon gang," said Seymour. "Let's leave this creep alone and go and have us some delicious "earthies"", (as they were known). Off the gang went, calling back names and taunting as they did so. They scurried down from the loft and out the barn door where Noah could see them from his perch on the window. He watched as they scampered and played about, finally disappearing from his view into the tall grass that surrounded a small pond where Farmer Boaz's cattle drank each evening.

Noah sat for a bit, blinking, his feelings very hurt. He would love to be part of that laughing, carefree group but it would have to be on his own terms and his alone. He could not and would not learn to play their games.

He had much to learn about mingling with others of his own kind not realizing that he would have to give a little, unbend from his stiff ways and superior attitude for his fellow mice to accept him as one of them.

Right now however, Noah was lonely and more importantly he was very hungry, the talk of "earthies" having made his mouth water. Hesitantly, he got up from his perch and very slowly followed the same route they had taken. Perhaps if he trailed along behind, he could find where they had gone and just perhaps, the place where the juicy earthies lived would be revealed. Along wandered Noah, his head lost in thoughts, until he found himself in amongst the tall grass that fringed the small pond. If he hadn't been daydreaming and keeping an eye out for "earthies", he might have noticed sharp little eyes and twitching little whiskers behind clumps of marsh grass and pond weeds. In a shaded open area Noah spotted what he thought were several "earthies" just waiting to be devoured. He jumped upon one quickly and bit into its ripe plumpness. To his horror, the earthy was the tail of a resting grass snake who, feeling the sharp sting from Noah's bite, uncoiled and doubled around to see what it was that had caused the pain. The grass snake reared up, her eyes flashing anger and at this moment, several of the other "earthies" moved and Noah realized that he was in the centre of a snake lair, a place where snakes hibernate and come out after the winter to bask in the sun before heading out for their summer wanderings. The snakes were a brilliant green in color, extra bright as they had just shed their winter skins. They were wide awake and very hungry. Now thoroughly roused up, the grass snakes surrounded Noah and began sliding, slithering toward him, mouths wide open, ready to devour a fat mouse, their first meal of the season.

"I saw him first!" called out one.

"No, I did," hissed another.

"Well he bit me, he should be mine!" spat the first snake.

"Mine!"

"No mine!"

"I saw him first."

"Quit crowding."

"Push off."

And the snakes began to fight and argue amongst themselves, hissing and crowding into one large angry ball of writhing snake flesh. Noah could not tell where one snake began and another ended. So angry at one another they had become, that they quite forgot about Noah who took the first opportunity to run, and run as he had never run before.

As he passed the pond grass clumps, the other mice that had been hiding there popped out.

"Who's smart now?" snickered Seymour.

"Serves you right," sneered others, but at that point, nothing more could be said as six angry snakes, now all uncoiled and boiling mad came roping and roiling out of the tall grass and all the mice, Noah included, raced for their lives back to the safety of the barn loft.

When they knew they were safe, Noah turned upon Seymour with anger, "You knew that there were snakes down by the pond, why did you lead me there?"

"To teach you a lesson," sneered Seymour.

"I could have been a snake supper," squeaked Noah, so outraged his voice almost left him. "You knew there were no "earthies" there."

"Well, what if we did?" replied Seymour, now beginning to feel just a bit ashamed at bullying this one defenceless little mouse. After all, he really had never done anything all that bad except turn up his snout at their little mouse games.

"Anyway," sniffed Lucy, another pal of Seymour's, "You weren't hurt were you, so quit whining." With that, Seymour and his friends scampered off to find their supper and left Noah hurt and confused, but perhaps a little wiser about setting himself so far apart from the others.

CHAPTER FOUR

In Which We Meet Snoad

NOW IT'S TIME TO explain the odd friendship that grew up between Snoad the farm cat and Noah. Snoad was a gray and battle-scarred old cat who lived in the barn loft. For many years, Snoad had been the sworn enemy of all mice, rats, voles and any of the smaller folk who live their lives in the barn or in the surrounding fields. One of the first lessons taught to any junior mouse was to beware of Snoad the cat; the cat who was as quick as lightning on his feet, with sharp razor claws and teeth designed to feast on young, unsuspecting mice. Snoad was just as mean and nasty as his claws were sharp. Lately however, Snoad seemed to be slowing down. He would spend long hours dozing in the loft windows, as though gazing listlessly upon the farm and all that went on there. In the evening, Farmer Boaz always left a saucer of milk for Snoad after his milking chores were over and this now seemed enough for him. Instead of spending the evenings chasing and hunting as before, now he seemed content to climb down the loft ladder to the milking stool, lap up the fresh foaming milk, hiss at the cows and then climb back up the ladder to the loft.

One evening, as Noah was making his unhappy way home from another day at school, he happened to be passing the ladder to the loft at the time that Snoad was about to climb up it. Noah of course ducked out of sight behind a clump of sweet smelling clover that was meant for the horses' supper. Noah's bright little eyes never left the cat's progress and he was most amazed to see the cat stop at the base of the ladder and look about. Usually Snoad would race to and bound up the ladder, eyes flashing, tail switching and tongue licking the last of the tasty milk still on the fur around his mouth. Yet today, Snoad's tail moved around slowly and his head turned from side to side looking very confused. Slowly he began to climb the ladder's steps . . . very slowly, and when he was almost at the top and about to leap from the steps into the barn loft, he lost his balance and, fell; fell with a very hard thump to the barn's cement floor where he lay unmoving.

Noah stared bewildered! Cats don't fall off ladders, cats are quick and savage, leaping, pouncing and racing about but this was right in front of him . . . a cat who had fallen off a ladder that he had climbed a thousand times. Noah didn't really know what to do; part of him told him to run home to safety, but another part told him to get nearer and find out what was wrong. A new thought from nowhere popped into his head; perhaps he could help his fallen enemy. Noah was curious and now concerned but was taking no chances and so he crept as closely as he could to the heap of gray fur. He kept his eyes on the lookout for the lightning slash of those razor claws but no, not this evening. Noticing that the fur on the cat's back was slowly rising and falling, he knew that Snoad was not dead. Now almost within reach of those fearful claws and that vicious mouth of fanglike teeth, Noah uttered a small and inquisitive squeak. Slowly the cat's eyes opened but remained unfocused, and now Noah could see the slight film over both of Snoad's once brilliant green eyes. The cat had become partially blind and could not see well enough to make the leaps and bounds he once did, landing on all four paws just where he had planned. Snoad was old and old age is not always kind to animals who live on Wild Wold Farm. When horses or cows became too old to work, Farmer Boaz would let them spend their days grazing in the back pasture, but there were no provisions made for an old cat beyond a saucer of milk each evening.

In a feeble voice Snoad asked, "Who is it that I can sense so near to me?"

"If I tell you will you promise not to harm me?" came the shaky and unsure reply.

"Who is it that dares to come so near?" hissed Snoad with something less than his usual forceful voice.

"It is I, Noah the mouse."

"Noah, the mouse? I'll have you for my supper!" snarled Snoad who attempted to rise but fell back. "I can't see and I can't move," he whined.

"I will help you and be your guide if you won't eat me," ventured Noah, sounding braver than he felt.

"How can a mere mouse morsel help me, the terror of the farm?" said Snoad, trying to sound a lot tougher than he felt.

Noah thought quickly. "Well, I could climb up on your back, sit between your ears and give you instructions as to which way to turn, or to let you know if a danger or some object is in the way."

"Danger? What possible danger could be in my way? This is Snoad you're speaking to, the terror of . . ."

"Yes, I know," returned Noah, growing weary of this. "The terror of the barnyard, but it looks to me that you could use my help."

Again the cat tried to rise up and did so, taking several steps forward and banging into the loft steps.

"Well, I'll just be on my way," said Noah, starting off.

"Wait just a minute," said Snoad, "perhaps we could come to some arrangement."

"And what would that be?" asked Noah, quite confident now that the poor cat did need him and just crafty enough to realize this might work to his advantage.

"Well, as you said, you could guide me. Of course, you must realize that this is only temporary until I get back to normal, which I'm sure won't be long."

"Of course," responded Noah, thinking to himself that it would be a long time before Snoad returned to normal. "And you must promise with an oath of honour that you will never harm me."

"Oh alright, I swear I won't," (or at least until I can see again, Snoad thought to himself).

With some hesitation, Noah climbed up the side of Snoad's body, feeling very awkward and a little nervous at this bold and daring thing he was doing.

Firmly settled between Snoad's two ears, Noah sat looking for all the world like an East Indian Emperor on his elephant. Noah felt the power and wonderful advantage of being carried everywhere he wanted to go and with such a marvellous view, that he had never had from mouse height. The two came to an arrangement by which, if Noah tweaked the left ear, Snoad was to turn left and right, if he tweaked the right ear.

Thus an odd but useful relationship was formed and while all the other mice were horrified at this, they realized that as long as Noah was in charge of Snoad's wanderings, there was less chance of one of them providing a tasty snack.

CHAPTER FIVE

Noah's First Big Adventure

MORE AND MORE, NOAH stayed away from Madame Topal at the school and, as there was no law that said he had to attend, he felt better just not being there, where he would be bullied and made fun of. He had begun roaming the farm, now that he had Snoad the cat to carry him wherever he wanted to go. He had learned at school that a mouse must always be on the lookout for hawks and owls, who were themselves always on the lookout for a quick snack of tender mouse.

This particular day Snoad was not feeling too well and preferred to remain in the barn saying, "You shouldn't go out in the daytime without me. Stay here and tell me stories."

But Noah, being wilful and liking his own way said, "No, I'm off to the banks of Sparkling Stream. If you want to spend this beautiful day inside, I'm off." Out he scurried into the sunny afternoon with not a cloud or a speck in the sky. He headed out across the meadow for the bank of Sparkling Stream. There it was shady and cool among the rocks and ferns that lined the shore. If you remember, it was the same Sparkling Stream that had turned into a raging torrent the night that Noah's Grandpa had to flee with his family to safety. Now though, the stream had gone back to being a winding little brook that made a pleasant bubbling sound, as it wound its way through the pasture and farmland. Noah reached the place among the ferns and rocks he particularly liked and stretched out letting all of nature's beauty surround him. He plucked a particularly deep shade of green leaf and used this as a hat to protect him from the sun. The world was full of color; the sky above was a deep blue space and all around him was the lovely emerald green of the various plants below, the clear water, through which could be seen the colourful rocks that lined the stream's bottom. Noah soaked in this natural beauty, his whole body in tune with the wonders of nature. He lay like this for some time, completely forgetting to do what every mouse must constantly do and that is, to look around for danger. Because of this carelessness the shadow that suddenly came between him and the golden sun, turned out to be a hunting hawk, who in a split second, had grasped Noah around his middle and was carrying him up, up and far above the farm.

Noah squealed in fright and utter amazement and, while his fear nearly paralysed him, he was able to notice the wonder of flight and of passing high above his home. Up, up, it seemed as though the hawk would never stop, but she was heading for a high distant tree where her two babies were waiting.

Many thoughts rushed through Noah's head, but he could think of nothing to get him out of this mess. Up, up, higher and higher flew the hawk, but on this afternoon, luck was on Noah's side. A small rabbit was lunching on some garden lettuce near the farm home and, as the hawk lifted higher, she spotted this with her super sharp eyes and thought, "While a mouse is tasty it's only a morsel, but a small rabbit could make a proper meal for my two young darlings." And thus the foolish rabbit, who should have known better, became the target for Mrs. Hawk. In a flash, she opened her talons and as she did, down fell Noah. Down he went like a stone, as the hawk also descended to clutch the startled rabbit around its plump middle and rise again to fly off to her nest with a very satisfied glint in her eye. Noah stumbled down, the sky and earth whirling around him, his tiny paws paddling helplessly. Thunk! He fell on his back into a very convenient rhubarb patch in that same garden that the late rabbit had been nibbling. The broad leaf of the rhubarb plant was weighted down with droplets of water from a recent shower. When Noah hit the leaf, the droplets flew into the air and the broad leaf shot up, catching Noah neatly like a baseball glove catches a fly ball.

Except for the shock of this whole experience, Noah was really none the worse for wear but when he later related the whole story to Snoad, he was not met with approval.

"I warned you. I told you no fool goes out in broad daylight larking about the meadow," Snoad grumbled. "Next time you do just as I tell you and stay with me."

While Noah did not particularly enjoy hearing Snoad tell him what to do, he was secretly pleased that his cat friend would even care.

CHAPTER SIX

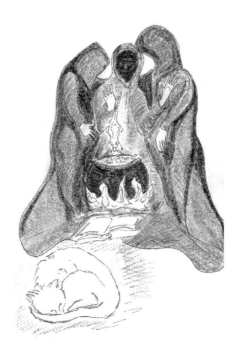

Snoad, Noah and Lamb's Tales

O N A WINDY COOL day in October, Noah and his friend Snoad were spending the afternoon in the sheltered area formed by the overhanging rocks down by Sparkling Stream. On this particular day, Snoad was feeling very sorry for himself. Snoad at the best of times was grumpy and snarly but Snoad depressed . . . well, it didn't make for pleasant companionship. Noah tried to cheer him up but Snoad would not be comforted.

"It's all very well for you to sit there and sympathize," snapped Snoad. "But until old age takes its toll on you, you have no idea what it is like to barely be able to see and to suffer the humiliation of having a mere mouse guide me about, and what's worse, I can't hunt and be the terrorizing tomcat of the farmyard anymore." Bitter tears ran down Snoad's cheeks, as he remembered the days when he stalked the farm, and all small and some not-so-small animals and birds were terrorized by him. "Do you remember those days?" whined Snoad. Noah didn't reply and tactfully did not mention how he and the other mice had had to run for their lives when Snoad was on the prowl. Noah did not let Snoad upset him with his sour observations when feeling badly and so Noah, the true friend that he was, he tried to think of ways to have fun.

"I know," chirped out Noah. "How about if I read you some adventure? If you can't have them at least you can hear about them, although I don't know where we can find the books with adventures in them." Snoad was doubtful about the whole idea and anyway, feeling sorry for himself was kind of pleasant in a negative sort of way.

"What about Farmer Boaz's house?" asked Noah. "You used to live there. You should know whether he has books or not."

Snoad sneered. "When I lived in the house I was petted and pampered. I spent my days in the kitchen on a cushion being fed treats by Mrs. Farmer Boaz. That was all before they decided to turn me out into the barn to work for a living. What an unhappy day that was for me! Can you imagine me, the petted darling of the house, having to make my home in the loft and exist upon whatever I could catch?" Snoad eyed Noah with something of his old hunting fire, but his clouded eyes could only make out an outline of Noah's little body and anyway he'd made an oath to protect Noah and never harm him. "Anyway," sniffed Snoad, "it was quite a comedown I assure you."

"But you could remember your way around the house now," Noah insisted.

"I suppose I could, although I did vow I'd never return." Noah was by now used to Snoad's aristocratic and prideful ways but he respected him. Although the relationship between them was really based on mutual need, Noah at least had begun to develop a true affection for the once masterful but now humbled cat.

"Well let's go and see what we can find," coaxed Noah. "We will never know until we try." In his heart, Noah was a little unsure at the prospect of entering a human's home. What if there were traps set just for inquisitive mice? What if . . . . but Snoad had reluctantly gotten to his feet. "Well, if we're going to do this, let's get going. Mrs. Farmer Boaz is usually out weeding her garden at this time of day, so the coast will be clear."

Noah climbed up onto Snoad's back and guided him to the farmhouse where they found the low kitchen window open. Noah was very nervous, although he was determined not to let Snoad know. He had never been inside a human house and had no idea what he might find there. His adventuresome nature took over at that point and he decided that this exploration would be an exciting episode.

Inside the house Noah was dazzled by the strange sights and smells. There were gleaming surfaces and shiny objects all quite different from the touch and textures of nature that he was familiar with. "I think it's all a little cold and hard," thought Noah. "I prefer the barn and meadow." From one room to another they wandered until Snoad found the place in the living room that he remembered.

"Over here," hissed Snoad, impatient with Noah's wonderment. Wide-eyed Noah scurried to Snoad's side.

"These are the books. Are there any here full of adventures?" Noah cocked his head and read the titles down the sides of the books backs: *Agricultural Principles, Raising Successful Sheep, Calves and How to Wean Them.* "These books don't seem to be full of any adventure; in fact they seemed downright boring unless you were a farmer. We aren't going to find any adventuresome reading here. Let's go back to Sparkling Stream and spend the rest of our day doing nothing."

"Wait!" said Snoad. "There are several more over there on that small table". Sure enough, partly hidden under some old newspapers were several books. These belonged to Farmer Boaz's son Daniel when he had been a schoolboy and they had been abandoned and moved from place to place ever since. Noah climbed up onto the table and read the titles: *Math for Junior Levels, Principles of Chemistry, Physics Facts.*

"Nothing here for us," said Noah.

"Here is one more," Snoad replied, moving newspapers and an old sweater aside with his paw.

"Lamb's Tales from Shakespeare", read Noah. "No, this is just another farming book. Let's go." Disappointed they moved to hop down from the table, but in doing so, they nudged the book and it fell to the floor. Noah and Snoad rapidly got down to the book and regarded it with wonder for there, in front of them, the book had, in falling, opened to a page on which was a picture of a dark and dismal cave. In the center of the picture were three beings clustered around a large iron kettle suspended over an open fire. All around them were frightening objects: hideous grinning skulls staring eyelessly with bared teeth; owls, bats and warty toads perched here and there about the cave, all rapt with attention at what was going on around the bubbling kettle. Noah and Snoad were awestruck for several moments, before Noah's active little mind had a very original idea.

"I want to know more about this and what is going on," he thought. Something greater than Noah had ever experienced exerted a tremendous pull on his imagination and he realized that if he could concentrate and imagine, imagine hard enough, he might be able to take part in whatever adventures there were to be found. Alas, poor Snoad did not possess very much imagination, and he soon became bored and promptly fell asleep beside the book. Not Noah. He climbed to the top of the open page becoming very still, his eyes crossing as he concentrated and imagined, concentrated and imagined; a strange sensation came over him, almost as if unseen fingers were prising open his mind to experience things outside his world. Slowly, ever so slowly, the page beneath him began to move, distances began to appear, objects took shape and sounds became distinct.

The three around the pot began to move about; their faces were too hideous for Noah to look at for long, because they were all wrinkled, weathered and dry with purpled lips hanging open, revealing yellow snaggled teeth. Noah drew back to hide from them and as he did so, he heard them chanting and saw that they were hurling different objects into the murky boiling pot.

"Eye of newt and toe of frog" Noah heard. He felt very alarmed. What kind of adventure was this that he could be in such great danger? As he watched, the flames underneath the kettle grew higher and changed color from orange to blue, green, red and then dazzling white. Strange sounds, whirrings, buzzings and hummings filled the room and the whole scene became one of fire, noise and confusion. Noah, very frightened, made a move to scamper further from sight but as he did so, bang! Three pairs of yellow bloodshot eyes revolved upon him.

"Wool of bat and tongue of dog," they shrilled. Noah made another move when three pairs of scabbed hands reached out for him and three croaking voices in unison howled, "Double, double toil and trouble, little mouse into the cauldron on the double." Noah's eyes bulged with fear, as he felt the grasping slimy touch of those claw-like hands upon him. He squealed in terror as they made to lift him into the waiting boiling pot but just at that very moment, Snoad, who lay beside the open book dreaming of long-past days of hunting, switched his tail in his dream and as he did so, he knocked poor helpless Noah out of the picture and into the next one, but this was no better. Noah landed on the blade of a sword that was about to be plunged into the throat of a man. The sword was drawn back in a quick motion, and Noah skidded along the flat of the blade and was flung out of the picture altogether.

He landed very hard and flat on his back. Out of breath and still very frightened by the terrible things going on in the book, he lay still for some moments before venturing a look to see if Snoad was nearby.

"You'll never believe what just happened to me," Noah squeaked out, his voice raspy and high-pitched.

Snoad opened one eye and yawned lazily.

"Tell me about it later but right now, hop on my back. We better make tracks before Mrs. Farmer Boaz gets back." With one terrified backward glance at the fright-filled book, Noah gratefully hopped onto Snoad's back and held on for dear life, as he directed him the way back out through the low open window and onto the grass below.

His thoughts were a jumble of confusion. Overwhelmed by the power of his imagination and where it could take him, he thought that the next time, he would be a little more careful about the books he tried to enter.

CHAPTER SEVEN

Noah and the Wheels of Progress

J UST BEYOND THE BED of Sparkling Stream which winds its pleasant and inviting path through Wild Wold Farm, lies a lovely and unused water meadow called Munificent Meadow. This was set aside as a preserve to encourage wildlife and vegetation to live and create a place for farm families in the neighbourhood to come and enjoy peace, harmony and to observe the wonderful workings of nature.

Many species of plant and animal life did live in the meadow and in the forest that surrounded it. The meadow was a favourite place for the barn mice to come in the late evening to picnic on wild grass seeds and ripe berries found lying under the clumps of bushes dotting the area. Although always on the lookout for hunting raptors, foxes, weasels and grass snakes, the mice would frolic in the pale moonlight and enjoy a holiday from the everyday world of the barn.

On a particularly warm and moon-bright summer evening, Noah and Snoad were making their cautious way across the meadow grass looking for the luscious currants that had ripened and were falling from their bushes. As usual, Noah was riding on Snoad's back, piloting him as they made their way through the tall grass, always keeping a wary eye open for danger. Just before they came to a clump of currant bushes that they knew had particularly ripe and sweet berries, they stumbled upon a sight that stopped them dead in their tracks. In an area that covered many square feet, the grass was ripped up, trampled and now lay dead on the ground. Huge mounds of sand and gravel were scattered about, beside which were gigantic machines, earth movers, backhoes and other monstrous objects of destruction.

Deep, water-filled ruts from the tires of the machines formed ugly, muddy scars that criss-crossed the area in front of them.

So against the perfect harmony of nature was this intrusion of man; so horrific, that the two animals were, at first, frightened, awed and then, after taking in the devastation, they became angry.

"What will become of Munificent Meadow?" wailed Noah. "What is all of this for, who has done it and why?"

The site was deserted, so Snoad and Noah wandered about dismayed taking everything in.

Something fluttering caught Noah's eye and, after making sure that danger was not near, he could see a bundle of papers lying beside a briefcase half-opened on the ground. Someone had very carelessly left this behind. Ever ready to show off his ability to read, Noah leapt off of Snoad's back and onto the pile of papers, whereupon he was immediately absorbed, reading, mumbling and figuring out what it was all about. Snoad, as usual, took this opportunity for a long catnap. By now, he was used to Noah and his odd ways.

"Wake me up when you're finished your snooping so we can do what we came to do, feast on berries." Noah grunted agreement half listening; he was too immersed in the fascinating papers he had found. Here were sheaves of papers showing pictures of buildings, homes, stores, factories. Along with these were bundles of diagrams, plants, engineering material that, as Noah read, could only mean one thing: Munificent Meadows was to be destroyed and the land turned into a community of homes, schools and commercial buildings. This shock sent shudders through Noah. Their precious meadow, so beloved of all natural folk and so beautified by the profusion of flowering trees and shrubs was to be completely destroyed. What could be done? What could one tiny insignificant mouse do? Even his powerful imagination could not stop the onrush of those gigantic machines that could, without effort, uproot trees and gouge deep scars in the untouched ground. Noah thought and thought, his tiny eyes glistening behind his gleaming specs. Evening became night and Snoad awoke, cross and out of sorts, because, all this time, Noah had done nothing but sit cross-legged on top of the overturned briefcase, pouring over graphs, scuttling in and out of sheets of paper covered with figures that meant nothing to Snoad.

"Thanks a lot," he snarled. "You got me all the way out here for a picnic and what do we do? I oversleep and you waste your time rustling through a pile of papers that belong to humans. Let's go back to the barn." And so they did, Noah silent and thoughtful all the while.

Noah said nothing more and, for several days, the routine of the farm was disturbed by the sound of giant earth movers, graders, plows and trucks along with the sharp smell of diesel exhaust. Noah now spent his days sitting in the triangular windows of the barn loft just staring straight ahead. From up here, he could see the progress of the building site. He could see the deep gashes made in the earth; the raw, bleeding wounds from the piles of uprooted soil with plants and trees lying about discarded and dying, their roots sticking into the air like arms calling for help. Still he sat and brooded. Even Snoad couldn't pry him from this spot with promises of picnics and maybe even adventures. Noah had some disturbing knowledge and he was thinking very hard about what to do with it. After three days of this had gone by, Noah sought out Snoad near the milk pails that were lined up alongside the barn wall. Snoad often hung around this area hoping for a quick snack, if Farmer Boaz should spill some of the delicious white fluid.

"Come with me," demanded Noah, "I have news and a plan and I, I mean we, need your help." Off they went to their favourite hiding place among the rocks and ferns alongside Sparkling Stream and here Noah explained to Snoad what he had read, what he had learned out in Munificent Meadow and what he could do about it. Snoad listened carefully. He had come to form a deep respect and love for his little pal. When Noah spoke, Snoad listened, as he knew that the little mouse usually had something well thought-out to say. For a long while, Noah spoke. Often Snoad would seem to argue and disagree but in the end he swished his tail several times and said, "I'll see what I can do, but don't forget, I'm old and these things take time."

"We don't have any time, so try to be as quick as you can, please, please!" And so for the next week Snoad could be seen in every corner of the farm talking to every being that he came across, even some, such as birds, that were usually too timid to talk to a cat, were seen listening carefully to what he said, although keeping a safe distance. Out in the fields, along the paths, down into the forest strolled Snoad spreading his word amongst all he could find and pleading with everyone to tell everyone else they saw or knew about the Big Plan of Action.

Exactly two weeks to the day after Noah and Snoad had discovered the building site, a wonderful and spectacular event took place. At precisely eight o'clock in the morning, just as the construction crew was arriving to begin their day's activities, the skies overhead were darkened by hordes of birds: robins, owls, sparrows, hawks, birds of every description flew in battle formation and headed straight for the construction site where they proceeded to dive at the men cowering there. Sparrows aimed their sharp little beaks at any exposed flesh they could find. Men had to hide their eyes behind their hands in order to protect them. Waves of eagles, hawks and owls let drop rocks that they could pick up with their claw-like feet, so that a rain of sharp stones hailed down. Robins and bluebirds darted in and out, relieving themselves upon the worksheets laid out for the day's activities. The men ran for cover and tried to hide from this onslaught from the air but this wasn't all. As the men tried to cover themselves, foxes came rushing out of the forest to nip at them, grass snakes formed themselves into loops to lasso and trip the men as they ran. Badgers hissed menacingly from pathways and the whole of Munificent Meadow became a moving battle ground, as every farmyard animal arrived to do his or her part in the fight. Horses galloped back and forth, trampling delicate surveying instruments. Ducks and geese ran in amongst fleeing legs to nip and peck. Barn bats flew low to grab at hats with their little claws. Turkeys and chickens set up such a clatter that, what with the neighing of horses, the bellowing of bulls, the day became one of mass confusion, noise and chaos.

The construction men who were big, burly fellows waved their arms and tried to ward off the pecks, bites and blows they received, but they were helpless against such a concentrated attack. They ran off into the forest shouting and panic-stricken at this turnabout in nature.

While all the noise and confusion of the main battle was going on, rats, voles, mice and squirrels, all little animals who gnaw and nibble with their sharp little teeth, set about chewing; chewing up any paper, canvas, rubber, or wooden part of the machines. Snails, grubs and slugs gladly gave up their lives by filling up gas and oil tanks to form a useless sludge.

As night drew on, a terrible silence fell over Munificent Meadow. Everywhere were the bodies of animals and birds who had perished in the battle, and everywhere was silence, as each bird and animal trembled in his nest or lair wondering at this bravery. Were they brave or merely foolhardy, had one small mouse led them into a terrible catastrophe? Would the world of humans return with vengeance to exact retribution for the destruction they had caused?

They shivered and wondered and worried all that night. They knew that humans could come with traps, poison and guns; they knew it could be their end.

Dawn brought a delegation of men in important looking suits to survey the damage. Machines wouldn't start, trucks wouldn't move, every moving part of every machine had been gnawed through or ripped to shreds. The men talked among themselves as storm clouds darkened the land and as a cold rain began to fall. Abruptly the men left. Those watching from nest and lair couldn't help noticing that the men walked slowly and dispiritedly. Several days later after rain had left pools of water and oceans of mud, great machines arrived, tearing up the earth and making a dreadful sound. At first the watchers thought that their efforts had been in vain and that the men were going to continue their work, but it soon became apparent that the new machines were being hitched up to the old ones and were hauling them away. After a day of this, everything had been removed and all that was left was an ugly scar in the centre of the meadow, a devastated area devoid of all life. Time would heal the scar as vegetation would cover it, nature always covering over the wounds done to the earth.

And what about our little hero during all of this upheaval? Our tiny mouse who had masterminded the entire event? Noah spent the day of battle in his usual perch on the barn loft's triangular windows, where he could watch the proceedings.

That night he curled up beside Grandpa Ezekiel with a small satisfied smile on his face.

From this time forward, Noah gained a new respect from the farm folk and particularly the mice.

They didn't exactly befriend him, as he was still stiff and aloof, but they treated him with respect and the best of all, the bullying stopped forever. Seymour and his gang treating Noah with awe and not a little wonder.

CHAPTER EIGHT

Goodbye to Snoad

N OAH WAS WORRIED ABOUT Snoad. Along with becoming increasingly snappish and cranky, Snoad just seemed to want to doze all day in a sun-warmed spot on the windows of the barn loft.

"Leave me alone," hissed Snoad whenever Noah suggested picnics or adventures.

"I just want to lie here and dream about when I was the catastrophic cat, the terrible tom of the barnyard," and then he would close his filmy eyes and doze off. Every once in a while his tail would twitch as he dreamed of mice, catching birds and other barnyard activities. Whether we approve of them or not, these ways are part of nature and not for us to judge. Noah shrugged and wandered off, more alone than ever without his usual companion upon whom he relied for transportation and protection. Theirs was a very special and unusual relationship. It started out with mutual need but as is so often the case, a loving trust began to grow between them. Although Snoad would probably rather go without his favourite milk (thoughtfully provided by Farmer Boaz) than admit it, but he loved and respected this odd little scrap of a mouse with his pompous ways and his flashing specs. Heaven forbid if Farmer Boaz's new farmyard cat, whose name was Claude should ever see the two together, Snoad would lose any respect he ever had. Claude was nastier, meaner and more unforgiving than Snoad could ever hope to have been. Perhaps it might be well to explain here that, after Farmer Boaz retired Snoad to a home in the barn and dishes of fresh milk, a new tomcat had wandered in one day. This new cat proceeded to take over Snoad's position of barnyard cat. Snoad was jealous of this young, slick feline who could run, jump, and prowl without any difficulties. He realized there was little he could do and so gratefully he accepted Farmer Boaz's retirement package.

Noah missed him each day that Snoad wished to remain indoors. They had spent many hours talking about life, having picnics or just lazing in the cool shade by Sparkling Stream. Noah began to read a great deal more on the garbage dump and took solitary rambles through Munificent Meadow, where one evening he met Yahoody, the hedgehog, but that's another story. Noah always felt truly alive out in Munificent Meadow. Here everything was in place with nothing to disturb or upset the balance. Nature pursued its course and Noah was at one with it. He loved to lie on his back on a rocky outcrop near "The Scar" and watch all that went on. The circling hawk high in the blue vault of the sky (upon whom he kept a wary eye), the busy ants beneath the grass cover as they lifted and carried objects many times their own weight to build their homes. By watching so carefully, Noah began to realize that from the smallest spider spinning its dainty web to the largest deer or fox, all living creatures were part of a great and wonderful working spirit. Each played its part to keep the whole of nature operational. If bees didn't spread pollen as they searched for nectar, then the clover would die and there would be no food for the deer who came to browse. Thus Noah learned great lessons.

One very rainy day, Noah was restless. Sitting in the barn loft with Snoad had proved futile as Snoad was just as grumpy as he could be that day and clearly wanted to be left alone. It was the kind of dreary, dismal day that Grandpa Ezekiel would call a "doley" day. It was too wet to spend time in Munificent Meadow or beside Sparkling Stream, Noah's usual haunts, or reading until his eyes stung and watered. He had become increasingly uncomfortable and so Noah wandered out of the barn into the yard beyond wondering what to do with himself. As he wandered about making sure his leaf hat was firmly in place to keep out the rain, his ears detected the distant rumble of automobiles along the highway that passed by Wild Wold Farm. He had never been the slightest bit interested in exploring the possibilities of this manmade road as he knew it would be noisy and dangerous. Today however was one of those days when it seemed better to do something rather than nothing and so Noah ambled through the wet grass until he reached the verge of the highway. Here it was as he had thought. Gigantic trucks and cars all racing frantically back and forth and Noah, from his roadside perch, took it all in with dismay. This wasn't nature's harmonious balance; this was effort and noise with no purpose or outcome that could possibly benefit his world. As he was lost in this kind of thought, a sudden gust of wind and rain passing by tore at his leaf hat and took it tumbling into the roadway and the young mouse without a second thought, after it.

Back at the barn, shortly after Noah had left, Snoad awakened and called out for him but realized that he had gone. Making his way painfully (with his arthritic joints) to the loft windows, Snoad could dimly see Noah disappear into the tall grass that led to the highway beyond. Feeling very badly about how he had snapped at his little friend, Snoad decided that, even though he wasn't feeling all that well, he would catch up and spend some time with him. He painfully got down the ladder of the barn loft and then let his ears guide him to the busy roadway. He emerged from the tall grass at the same instant that Noah dashed across the highway after his hat. Snoad understood in an instant what would happen. Noah, unused to road traffic, would be flattened unless he acted. With one mighty and tremendous gathering of every muscle and sinew he possessed, old Snoad leapt onto the roadway catching Noah neatly in his paws. In one shining moment, Snoad recaptured the days of his youth and his prime but at that same instant, an oncoming car hit him squarely sideways. Flying through the air both Snoad and Noah sailed to the other side of the road where they fell in a heap in the rain-soaked ditch. For the longest time, nothing could be heard but the rattle and drone of the passing traffic and the occasional patter of wind-driven rain on the grass. Finally a very small voice squeaked, "Snoad? Snoad? Are you okay?" There was no answer. Painfully, for Noah was bruised from head to toe, he made his way over to where Snoad lay. The cat's sides were moving up and down very slowly so Noah knew he was still alive. Noah crept up to Snoad's face, their whiskers just touching, and he looked into Snoad's dim eyes that were beginning to close.

"Thank you Snoad," whispered Noah and Snoad's paw moved ever so slightly to rest on Noah.

"You're welcome," came the barely heard response.

"I love you Snoad," said Noah.

"Me too," came the response.

And they both lay there for a long time as Snoad breathed his last breath, remembering picnics and adventures, battles on the meadow and long talks by Sparkling Stream.

CHAPTER NINE

Noah Meets Mrs. Yahoody

ABOUT SIX MONTHS OR so after the meadow battle (as it was referred to by the barn animals), the terrible scars left by the machines were pretty well covered by grass, weeds and shrubs. If anything, the scars had made small hills and valleys for the smaller meadow folk to hide in and remove themselves from the ever eager eyes of hungry hawks and owls. Noah spent more and more time out in the meadow, even during the day when he had been warned repeatedly by other mice that it was dangerous no matter how careful he might be. Noah of course knew it all, just shrugged his shoulders saying:, "Oh, you're just jealous because I might have some exciting adventures while you are back here in the stuffy old barn playing silly games of Hide-and-Seed and anyway, old lady Topal hates me!" (Noah was not often disrespectful but he made an exception when it came to Madame Topal).

"Go on then, get eaten by hawks, who cares," said Seymour as Madame Topal entered the school area.

"Do not play with that naughty, heedless mouse!" she cautioned. "He'll come to no good, you'll see. Stay away from him."

"But he saved the meadow," said Dorcas, a very pretty, petite brown mouse, who secretly had a bit of a crush on our Noah and would have loved to have shared in some of the picnics he always talked about.

"That is true," replied Madame Topal. "And for that we are all grateful. But I'm here to teach you all the rules of Mousedom and you must learn them for your own future and safety." With a sharp snap of her tiny teeth and a glare from her black little eyes, she brought the class to order.

"Now let's get on with our camouflage lesson."

Thus the lovely little Dorcas joined the others in a lesson about how to sit very still and blend with surroundings. Noah shrugged again, pretending not to care, and sauntered into the open barnyard. Since Snoad's death, he was on his own and unprotected, but he told himself he wasn't afraid, he could read and most of all he had single-pawedly saved the meadow from destruction. This turned out to be Noah's lucky day, as the clear blue sky held not a speck which could so easily turn out to be an eagle or other bird of prey hoping for a juicy mouse snack. To the meadow Noah strolled, his little specs flashing and his tiny chest puffed up with pride. It was his meadow and he was going to enjoy it. After all he had saved it, hadn't he? He picked his careless way through the waving grass and wild field flowers, stopping occasionally to smell them or snack on some particularly succulent seeds that he found scattered about. Humming a tuneless little song that sounded like the buzz of bees and the soughing of the wind, Noah made his way to the center of the meadow. When he reached the area of the scar he thought, "I'll just lie on my back, gaze at that blue sky and dream." He was making himself comfortable on a particularly inviting little hummock of grass. Turning on his back and stretching luxuriously out, he let the sun warm him from the tip of his black shiny little nose to the other tip of his black little tail. Suddenly he was rudely bounced into the air, his back prickling with what seemed like small needles. He righted himself and turned to stare in the direction of the hastily vacated spot. The spot seemed to move and from beneath the matted underlay of dead grasses, there emerged the most curious looking animal that Noah had ever seen.

"Just who do you think you are and what do you think you are doing?" demanded this tiny creature, its very sharp and needle-like nose twitching angrily. Noah was quite taken aback and for several moments could only stare in disbelief. "Well?" demanded the creature. "Are you going to stand there all day staring? Don't you know it's rude?" The creature huffed and puffed itself into a round ball of prickles. "Don't you realize you are upsetting our afternoon snooze?"

"I, I, well, I'm sorry," stuttered Noah. Although he was a prideful and heedless little mouse, he was a gentle one, who would never knowingly harm or disturb anyone.

"Well, sorry just isn't good enough and anyway, what are you, a barnyard mouse, doing out here in my meadow patch?"

"Your meadow patch?" echoed Noah. "This is called Munificent Meadow." He was beginning to become a little annoyed at this creature's attitude. After all, he had apologized, hadn't he? And now this "my meadow" bit was too much to swallow. "Now see here you . . . whatever you are. This meadow, which I, by the way, saved from destruction, belongs to all of nature folk and who, or should I say, what are you?"

The tiny creature now came out from under the overhanging mat of grass where she had been hidden and Noah could see that she was a round ball of spiny, thorn-like spikes with two tiny eyes and a very pointed nose.

"Who am I? I am Mrs. Yahoody and I'm a hedgehog. I live amongst shrubs and bushes, but I thought that this area was particularly attractive so I decided to make it my own".

"Your own? Well I think not," snapped a by now thoroughly annoyed Noah. "We nature folk have fought and died to keep this meadow for our own and we aren't about to let you scuttle in here and lay claim to it all".

The force of Noah's anger came through in his high-pitched squeak and the hedgehog backed away a bit considering this, finally saying "Are you that know-it-all mouse that I've heard so much about? The one that organized all the nature folk here to rise up against the construction men and get rid of them in a huge battle?"

"Well, I guess I'm the one," sniffed Noah, not knowing whether or not to be insulted by being called a know-it-all.

"Well, in that case, welcome," said the hedgehog, "and come out everybody." At this, to Noah's surprise, out shuffled six more even tinier quilled hedgehogs. "This is my family and we've come to make our home in these parts."

By now Noah was totally intrigued by these new and interesting little animals with their beady eyes, pointy noses, twitching armoured bodies and softly furred bellies. Noah thought them very attractive and interesting.

"Tell me about yourself," said Noah.

"I will if you do likewise," replied Mrs. Yahoody. "You all go back into the den to finish your afternoon naps." Obediently, the other tiny hedgehogs disappeared beneath the grassy overhang that was to have been Noah's resting place.

"Now about us. We hedgehogs hunt for earthies and grubs in the evening and I want the young ones to be well-rested," said Mrs. Yahoody. She took up a comfortable spot in the shade of a currant bush and Noah made himself a spot nearby. "Well, we heard about this meadow and how all of nature was welcomed here, and that we could live our lives peacefully without fear."

"There are predators all about," interrupted Noah.

"Yes, yes, I know, naturally they are all everywhere, but here, as long as we are cautious and take care, we shouldn't have to worry too much."

Noah thought about what had been said to him that morning about taking care, but he pushed that thought out of his mind.

"We," continued Mrs. Yahoody, "lived near a town and were constantly being bothered by the noise of humans tramping about so

I packed up the kiddies and set out for here. Munificent Meadow . . . what does that mean?" she asked.

"It means bounteous, generous, rich and gift-giving," replied Noah, ever ready to show off his knowledge. "And with all this bounty, there is always danger all around," beginning to sound to himself like Madame Topal.

"I told you that I'm aware of that, heavens, I haven't raised four broods for nothing but that doesn't take away from the peace and beauty of this . . . what you call Mun . . ."

"Munificent Meadow" finished Noah graciously, and Mrs. Yahoody went on giving details of her life. Noah was beginning to like and respect his new prickly little friend. He was in greater need for friendship than he realized. The passing of Snoad had left a very vacant spot in his heart.

"Now, tell me your story," asked Mrs. Yahoody. "I've heard about how you saved the meadow, but there must be more." Noah loved to talk about himself, however seldom he found anyone who would listen. He told the exciting story of how his Grandpa Ezekiel had saved him during the terrible flood and of his adventures after that.

"Where is Grandpa Ezekiel now?" asked Mrs. Yahoody.

"He is home, he is always there waiting for me. I think sometimes that he worries about me, he feels that I'm too independent and that I should try to fit in more with the other mice."

"Well, I won't argue with that but, you strike me as being a pretty level-headed guy from what I've seen," replied Mrs. Yahoody. Noah swelled with gratitude; he liked to be flattered and to tell the truth, it was good for him to be admired by someone.

The shadows had lengthened without the two storytellers noticing and soon evening had arrived. The sun was sinking in the west leaving a lovely, hazy glow on the land.

"Do you want to come hunting for earthies and slugs with us?" asked Mrs. Yahoody,

Noah, who loved earthies above all else, answered, "Yes, I'd like to come. I know where there are some particularly fat earthies down by a swampy area not far."

Mrs. Yahoody uttered a shrill high note and, as if they were waiting for a signal, out tumbled the six tiny hedgehogs and off the eight went, the sun going down, making their bodies cast long shadows on the grass. No one noticed an even longer and larger shadow that trailed along behind them. Foxes like to hunt in the evening also and this particular fox had two cubs back in a lair at the edge of the woods who were hungrily awaiting her return.

Noah and Mrs. Yahoody rambled on, first one and then the other talking non-stop about life and adventures. So busy were these two new friends concentrating on one another's stories and so fast were the six tiny hedgehogs trying to catch up that Mrs. Yahoody completely forgot her own words telling of her care and attention to caution that no one noticed when the long shadow trailing behind them began to catch up and overtake. Suddenly a full grown red fox sprang into the grass in front of Noah and Mrs. Yahoody, and they were cut off in mid-sentence. For several seconds no one moved and then, in a split moment everything became motion and a blur until all motion stopped and a scene of horror unfolded. The fox stood triumphant with one plump little mouse squirming in her jaws. The fox turned tail and began trotting off toward its lair.

Quickly one, two, three, four, five, six counted Mrs. Yahoody, making sure that her brood was safe, as they crept out from any bush or rock they had hidden under.

"All of you stay put right here and do not move until I return". After making sure her little ones were well hidden she scuttled off after the fox as fast as her short legs would take her. In time, she caught up with Mrs. Fox who was idling along, enjoying the lovely evening.

Mrs. Yahoody caught the eye of Noah who was wedged firmly between Mrs. Fox's upper and lower jaws. Mrs. Fox spotted Mrs. Yahoody and foolishly gave chase, and this fell into Mrs. Yahoody's plan perfectly. She would lead the fox into the swamp. Bobbing and weaving along with Mrs. Fox in hot pursuit, Mrs. Yahoody bravely led on. The bushes and grasses grew thicker and the soil more moist beneath their feet. Mrs. Fox, who was much heavier than Mrs. Yahoody, began to sink into the mud. So busy was Mrs. Fox in concentrating on getting out of danger that her grip loosened on poor Noah who found the breath to squeak out, "Oh please Mrs. Fox if you let me go, I'll show you the way out of this swamp." At first

Mrs. Fox ignored this plea but, as night was upon them and she no longer knew where she was, she dropped Noah from her mouth to the ground below but firmly held him with one paw.

She said, "Why should I trust you, my evening meal? If I let you go you will just run off and leave me to sink into this awful mud."

"No I won't," shrilled a by now, very shaken up and mauled little mouse. "I'm Noah and I'm good for my word."

"Oh, are you that smart mouse that saved Munificent Meadow from destruction?" asked Mrs. Fox in a somewhat kinder voice.

"Yes, I am he. Please, please let me go and I'll show you the way out."

Mrs. Fox thought for a bit; thought first about what a tasty morsel she had and then thought about her two lonely cubs left behind if she couldn't get out of this swamp. Sensing her hesitation, Noah renewed his heartfelt pleas. Mrs. Fox thought some more about how foolish she had been to chase a hedgehog which she couldn't eat anyway because of its spines and how she had ignored all of her life's teachings.

"Are you sure you are that little mouse who can read?" she asked.

"Oh yes, and can't you see how we are sinking in the mud?" wailed a filthy and wet Noah from beneath her paw.

"Very well," said Mrs. Fox who raised her paw with a squelch from the mud. "Show me the way out and I'll never bother you again".

Noah didn't have to be asked twice. He nodded to Mrs. Yahoody, who had joined several curious turtles and was watching all of this from a partially submerged log. Up the slope Noah made his muddy way followed by a grateful Mrs. Fox, and Mrs. Yahoody followed also, keeping a safe distance. When she reached the spot where her six babies patiently waited she waved to Noah, "I'll see you soon, please come and visit me again."

"I will," panted Noah.

When they reached the scar, Noah scurried off to the top of a rock where he felt safe and shouted to Mrs. Fox, "Now you know where you are and don't forget your promise!"

"I'll not forget and thank you," replied Mrs. Fox, surprised at her own kindly attitude which was most un-fox like. There was something about that mouse and while Mrs. Fox wasn't given to great gusts of inner thought, she did realize that that tiny animal had, in the end, saved her from her own foolishness. As she trotted off home, she glanced back at him and saw, or thought she saw, a strange glow about the little mouse sitting alone on the top of a rock in the moonlight.

CHAPTER TEN

Noah, Finding Love . . . . and Trouble

DORCAS WAS A VERY small, dainty mouse who had a style all her own. She was very pretty with sleek, shining fur and a very busy and flirtatious tail that would flick back and forth or stand straight up when she was excited or curious.

This little mouse was quite different from all the other members of her school group. While she happily entered into all of the games and always sat with polite attention to Madame Topal's lessons, there was something about her that set her apart. Perhaps it was a mischievous attitude, eyes always flashing with excitement at the idea of a picnic or a nature ramble. Dorcas secretly felt she liked Noah a lot. He had adventures and wasn't like the other mice, who were all much alike and did just what they were told, which she found boring.

When the other mice teased Noah, she would say nothing, secretly wishing she could get to know him better. Her chance came one day when Madame Topal was pairing the class up to practice Cat and Mousenapping techniques. This exercise was to fit the young mice out to avoid capture by a prowling cat. One mouse would play the cat, the other the mouse and try outwitting one another. No one wanted to be Noah's partner. This one day Noah had decided he had nothing better to do than attend class.

Seymour Mouse said, "Why would he want to avoid cats? We all know he used to hang around with Snoad, how crazy can you get?"

Dorcas who had watched and knew about Noah and Snoad's odd friendship volunteered, "I'll be Noah's partner, Madame Topal."

"Alright dear, if you are sure," replied Madame Topal. Dorcas was one of her favourites. Together Noah and Dorcas scurried down the loft ladder to the barn below where they had been sent to practice.

When they reached the bottom rung, Dorcas said, "Noah is it really true about you going out to Munificent Meadow on your very own in the daytime?"

"Yes," replied Noah who, by the way, was flattered to be paired with Dorcas, whom he had admired for some time. "Yes, I do, or I used to go with Snoad, did you know him?"

"Yes," shivered Dorcas, "I did, but wasn't he dangerous?"

"Oh no, not to me. You see, I was his eyes, he couldn't do without me." Noah was not above a little bragging upon occasion and this occasion seemed to call for it.

Noah paused. "Would you like to go to the meadow this afternoon? We could go to the scar, meet Mrs. Yahoody, my friend, and play with her six babies, or we could hunt for wild strawberries, would you like to?"

Dorcas would like to very much but her upbringing encouraged her to be cautious. "What about hawks, snakes and foxes?" she asked.

"Oh don't worry," said Noah airily. "I'll cover that problem—just come, it'll be fun."

And so Dorcas, who had never misbehaved, threw caution to the wind and said, "Oh yes, let's go, I have wanted to for so long." So they set off but not before Madame Topal, who had come down the ladder to check on her pupils' progress, had overheard them.

"I'll show those two" she said to herself. "And that Dorcas! Who would have thought that she, of all my pupils, would be heedless. It's all that Noah's fault; luring her off with promises of empty fun when they should be learning."

Madame Topal, who was very wise in the ways of daytime outdoor travel, began to follow the two, all the while talking to herself about what she would do when she caught up with them.

Noah and Dorcas wandered along the tiny path used by all of the smaller meadow animals. Noah loved showing off all the glories of the outdoors to Dorcas who was eager to take it all in; so excited was she by the thrill of playing hooky from school and having a real, live adventure. Noah showed Dorcas the flowers, the bees gathering pollen, tiny meadow voles and moles that they met along the way. When a hawk hovered overhead, Dorcas squeaked in fear, but Noah knew of a protective fallen branch nearby under which they could hide.

The sight of this same hunting hawk caused Madame Topal to also run for cover and, in doing so, she lost the trail of the naughty two and as they set off in one direction, she set off in another. Madame Topal knew the meadow well and she thought that even though she had lost sight of Noah and Dorcas, they would eventually turn up at the Scar, as it was usually the place where everyone, sooner or later arrived. The sun was very hot and as there was not a cloud in the sky, Madame Topal was soon out of breath and very warm. Coming into a clump of currant bushes, she sat down to gather herself and cool down. Madame Topal was not herself. In her anger at Noah and Dorcas, she had left a classroom of mice, she had got herself turned around, she was hot, tired, thirsty and hungry. A stray breeze brought to Madame Topal's little nose a very enticing smell. It was the smell of ripe currant berries but something more . . . the smell was so inviting that she left the bush she was under to track it down. Beneath another currant bush lay a heap of glistening berries, shining in the sun. Bees and wasps were busy at this pile of ruby red berries and Madame Topal soon found herself greedily filling herself with the tasty treat. These berries had fallen off the bushes and had lain in the sun for several days; the heat fermenting the juices in the little red globes and turning it to alcohol. Madame Topal had had a very strict upbringing and had not had much experience with the methods of relaxing and enjoyment. Thus she gorged on these fermented berries and, after having done so, felt very woozy and sleepy, but no matter what, her duty was to find the two upstart mice and so she set off zigzagging from left to right and singing a little mouse tune to herself as she did so. Madame Topal was drunk.

The two errant, young mice found the scar, picnicked on lovely fresh field strawberries, played with Mrs. Yahoody's six babies and just enjoyed a wonderful day outdoors. Dorcas loved to hear stories of Noah in various adventures.

As the sun showed signs of beginning to go down in the west Noah said, ``We had better get back to the barn—we don`t want to be late."

Dorcas, who felt she had grown to really like this dashing young mouse who told such wonderful stories of adventures, put her paw in his and together they made their way back to the barn.

That night there was to be a great gathering of all the mouse families in the loft. There were to be speeches, prize-giving and achievement cards for various mouse techniques to be given out.

Noah and Dorcas arrived back just in time to take a place in the rear of the assembly. Mouse after mouse stood up to give speeches about various aspects of mouse life, and finally the prize-giving time arrived.

Seymour's father, a large and important-looking gray mouse stood up and said, "It is time to give out the school prizes for the different subjects taught at our mouse school. I would like to ask Madame Topal, our teacher, to announce the prizes." There was silence for a while. "Madame Topal," said Seymour's father. After a long while during which there was whispering and rustling, a hiccup was heard from the back of the barn. All heads turned as Madame Topal, full of muddy streaks, her fur disarrayed, full of burrs and straw sticking out from behind her ears, lurched to the front of the gathered mice—stopped, stifled a giggle and promptly fell on her back, her four paws sticking helplessly into the air. The gathered mice were thunderstruck with horror – Madame Topal drunk before the entire barn mouse gathering. Several father mice rushed to the front to help Madame Topal to her feet. She left between the two of them, waving happily and hiccupping steadily.

Seymour's father took to the front again and silenced the buzzing crowd. "Well, ahem, most unusual behaviour, um, well, I wonder if it was part of some mouse behaviour techniques."

"She was drunk!" "Fire her!" "Bad example!" "Our poor children!" "What will they think!" "Shocking!" "Not to be tolerated!" Those and many other comments, filled the area until, after a whispered conversation with several other father mice, Seymour's father again took the floor.

"Silence please, we have discussed this among ourselves and we have decided upon Madame Topal's immediate dismissal."

This was met with sounds of approval and paw-clapping. Noah and Dorcas were listening to all of this, and Noah suddenly realized that perhaps this all had something to do with him and his taking Dorcas to Munificent Meadow that day.

He did not sleep well that night. And the next day, with a great deal of fear, he went to Madame Topal's nest which was in the wall near to the school area.

Madame Topal was not well; her little black eyes were bleary, she had tried to tidy herself up but she still looked bedraggled.

"I suppose you've come to sneer" she said. "Fired, after all I've tried to do, the work I've done and all because of you—you ingrate you, you!"

Noah let her squeak out her anger but when she was finished and panting, he said quietly, "Madame Topal, I know we haven't gotten along, I know that you don't like me and I know that a lot of it is my fault. Yesterday I led Dorcas to skip school and you followed us to try and bring us back. I'm going to Seymour's father to tell him the truth." And before the startled Madame Topal could breathe a word, he was off.

He quickly found Seymour's father who was busy directing a group of mice fathers on how they could better defend themselves by being a more organized force against predators.

Noah politely asked Mr. Seymour if he could have a word with him.

"I'm very busy and anyway, it is the likes of you that put us all in danger," replied Mr. Seymour in a very harsh voice.

"Hear, hear!" murmured many of the men mice.

Noah swallowed but decided to speak his piece, "Yesterday was not Madame Topal's fault," he began, "it was mine. She shouldn't be punished." He began to gain courage as he went along. "Madame Topal was doing her duty. She is hard-working and she really cares very deeply about what happens to all of us at the school. I led Dorcas away on a picnic." At this point Dorcas' father, who hadn't known about his daughter playing truant, became very angry.

"Why you little whippersnapper, I'll have your tail tied into so many knots you'll never undo them! You touch my daughter and I'll . . ."

He was stopped by Mr. Seymour who said, "Let him finish before we decide what to do with him."

Noah continued looking straight at Dorcas' father as he spoke, "As I said, it was all my fault, I promised Dorcas a picnic, that's all we did and we visited my friend Mrs. Yahoody out by the scar."

"A likely story," scoffed Dorcas' father.

"It's true and Madame Topal was following us to fetch us back and to watch over us. She got turned around and got mixed up under a currant bush."

"Under a currant bush indeed," muttered several of the mice men.

Noah continued, "It was hot and she was tired and confused, but she was only doing her duty."

The men discussed this among themselves for awhile. Several were heard to maintain that it was easy to mistake fermented berries for fresh ones. Several talked about Madame Topal's long years of devoted service. Finally Mr. Seymour said, "All right, Noah, thank you for your defence of Madame Topal, you have done the right thing. We have decided to give her back her job and not mention the ah, events of last evening."

Noah was overjoyed and vowed to himself that he would try very hard to at least respect Madame Topal in the future even if he knew they would never be friends.

He felt very good about himself knowing that he had done the right thing. When he next saw Dorcas, her eyes were shining with devotion and he knew he had made a true friend.

CHAPTER ELEVEN

Noah and the Lilly Pads

D URING HIS WANDERINGS ABOUT Wild Wold Farm, Noah had come
across a new and delightful place to spend time and explore.
It was a small pond called Lilypad Pond that had been created by
Farmer Boaz by damming up Sparkling Stream. This created a quiet
pool of water in a natural bend in the stream shaded by tall willows
and old oak trees. The result was a restful, quiet refuge for field

and woodland wildlife alike; a place for them to drink, rest and feel reasonably safe from the ever watchful eyes of predators, such as the constantly circling hawks & other raptors. The surface of the pond was just like a mirror reflecting the deep blue if the sky and the green of the overhanging willows, whose deep bending branches swept the surface of the tranquil water. Noah came upon this lovely setting one day after hearing from Mrs. Yahudi, his hedgehog friend, about a place not far from Munificent Meadow, where he could meet new friends and observe the wonders of nature. He arrived one afternoon when the sun was a large orange ball overhead. He had brought with him a picnic lunch of oats that he had packed into his cheeks for storage and a folded piece of paper taken the farm's rubbish heap. The paper was an article chewed from a magazine and it was about fascinating countries far away such as Egypt and China. Noah liked to learn, although he didn't like to go to school and always found excuses to be elsewhere. After he arrived at the pond, he found a shady spot on a large rock that rose half in and half out of the water. Arranging himself carefully on the top of the rock so that he could see all around him, Noah settled down to read and chew his snack. He had just finished a story about pyramids in far off Egypt, when he heard a sharp whistle nearby. Instantly alert for danger or for adventure, Noah's sharp little eyes surveyed the surrounding area, finally resting on one of the oddest animals that he had ever seen. It half rose up out of the water with its short, webbed feet resting on the rock and it's long, narrow body remaining half in the water. It had small, bright little eyes set on either side of its bewhiskered face. Its tiny ears grew close to a narrow head. The whole body was covered in wet, brown fur plastered flat. Noah stared in frank amazement, as he had never before known of an animal, besides ducks and geese, which lived in water. So complete was his amazement, that he quite forgot caution and squeaked out a startled, "What's that?"

The animal immediately spotted Noah and in a high pitched whistling voice said, "Just what are you staring at insignificant mouse who can't even swim?"

"I, well nothing really, it's just that you are all . . . well, wet," finished lamely.

"Well of course I'm wet you dummy I'm an otter and we live in and around water don't you know anything?"

Noah stiffened up a little at this. He did not like being called a dummy and certainly not by this half drowned animal whom he had never seen before.

"Yes, I know a good many things and most of all, I know when to be polite to strangers."

The animal had, by now, crawled up out of the water and was preening himself and drying his beautiful, rich brown coat of fur in the hot sunlight.

"Well I'm sorry I'm sure if I've upset you no need to take offense you know this is what I call my drying rock and I'm not used to strangers sharing it with me however you are welcome if you don't mind me drying and seeing to my coat it has to be taken care of you know."

The otter spoke in a continuous sentence without stopping for a breath and Noah wondered why, but didn't like to ask just yet. He remembered his manners that Grandpa Ezekiel had taught him and said, "I'm Noah and I live in the barn at Wild Wold farm. I was told about this wonderful spot on Sparkling Stream, and so I thought I would explore the area and bring a picnic lunch. I hope that you don't mind."

"Well no I suppose it's alright as long as you don't bother me with a lot of silly questions and anyway what's a barn mouse doing out here in the middle of the day shouldn't you be stealing grain from the farmer or something mouse-like?"

"I don't steal," replied Noah with some anger. "And anyway, Farmer Boaz is kind and generous, he begrudges us wild ones the bits of food we eat." A sudden idea hit Noah. "And what do you eat?" he asked politely.

"Why I eat fish naturally," replied the otter. "Why would you ask?"

"Because it occurred to me that you are as guilty of stealing Farmer Boaz's food as I am. He keeps fish in this pond to help feed his family."

The otter considered this for a brief moment and then swiftly changed the subject. "What did you say your name was mouse?" he asked.

"My name is Noah and I am pleased to meet you. What is your name?"

"I am known to my friends and family as Giles," answered the animal, "and I'm a river otter."

By this time, the animal had finished drying and combing his fur and, with a sudden flick of his tail, he disappeared under the surface of the water. Before Noah could even blink, the sleek and shiny animal had resurfaced and climbed back up the rock to where he had just been sitting not moments before.

"There what did you think of that pretty fast aren't I?"

Noah let his breath out in a gasp. "I should say you are," he said admiringly. "It must be wonderful to be able to swim and dive and to move so quickly."

The otter swelled a little with such praise and admiration and his attitude toward Noah began to change ever so slightly to one of a warmer and friendly sort.

"I could maybe teach you to swim and dive," he offered generously. "Of course you could never hope to be as good as I am."

Noah hastily thanked him but refused politely saying, "I don't think mice were meant to swim and dive."

He had forgotten the story of how Grandpa Ezekiel had had to both swim and dive when forced to the night of the flood, in which all of his family, except baby Noah, had drowned. Noah was too young to remember, but his Grandpa had often told him the story and how they had found refuge in a church and how Noah had learned to read and understand human language.

"Well if you can't swim and dive what can you do?" asked Giles

"Well, I can tell really interesting stories about far off places," said Noah. He did not think it was the right time to tell his new friend about his extraordinary abilities.

"That might be fun," replied Giles. "Can you tell one now I just have a bit of time before I have to fish for my supper you know the best time is late afternoon when the sun is lower and the fish come up from the deeper parts of the pond where they hide during the heat of the day so do you have a fast story to tell me or not?"

By now, Noah had become used to Giles' seemingly abrupt and rude ways and realized to himself that the otter was perhaps lonely and really would like to make a friend of him.

"Well yes, I do have a story to tell that you might find interesting."

With that, Noah started to tell the story about he had befriended the cat Snoad and of their adventures together until Snoad's sad death while saving Noah's life.

The otter became so interested that he quite forgot his grooming and fixed Noah with an unblinking stare, until he had finished his story.

"Well," he said, "you aren't the usual mouse one meets around here are you?"

There was a new tone of admiration in his voice. It seemed as though Giles needed to be convinced that someone was worthy of his trust and admiration, before he committed himself to a friendship.

"I have to go now," he said. "Can you come back tomorrow and tell me more stories"?

"Maybe I can," replied Noah. "If the weather is nice, I'll be back. Do you mind if I bring a friend?"

Immediately the otter was on his guard, cold and suspicious. "What do you mean friend what kind of friend who is it is it another mouse I don't want to overrun with mice here you know."

Noah hastened to assure the otter that he would not bring anyone that would threaten or upset him. "It is a friend of mine who doesn't get to go out and have many adventures. She has a very strict father and he keeps his eye on her all the time." Noah did not tell Giles about the time that he and Dorcus were playing hooky from school and got into so much trouble.

"Is she your girlfriend?" asked Giles abruptly.

Noah looked downward and if a mouse could ever blush, it would have been him. "Well, I don't . . . . ," stammered the little mouse, who was really quite shy about such things and had never really thought about Dorcas that way, although now it came to him that she really was a pretty little thing, and that he did enjoy her company more than any other. "I don't know about that, but she is very shy and won't bother you at all."

"Well if you're sure bring her along it will be alright as long as you have lots of good stories to tell." With that the otter flipped himself into the water with a splash that soaked Noah through.

After drying himself in the sun, Noah left to go back to his home in the barn and on his way, he met a group of mice his own age, and among them was Dorcas. They had all been out with Madame Topal, the teacher at mouse school. Noah seldom ever went to school, he didn't fit in with the others too well and he felt that he could learn all he needed to know on his own, using his extraordinary abilities to read and understand human language.

The first one to spot Noah was his old adversary Seymour, a large and athletic mouse who used to bully Noah but had stopped after Noah had proven himself a hero, when he saved Munificent Meadow from the human developers. Now, while Seymour didn't exactly consider Noah a near and dear buddy, he, at least, kept silent when Noah was around. This time however, he looked quickly around to see if Madame Topal was listening and, finding that she was occupied elsewhere, hissed nastily in Noah's ear, "Just make sure that you keep away from Dorcas, you nimwit mouse who hangs around with cats. Do you hear me?"

"Yes, I hear you and I'll hang around with just whom I please, be it cats or Dorcas, and if you don't like it, you can just lump it."

Noah surprised himself at his own courage but it certainly seemed to work as Seymour sidled off looking sheepishly over his shoulder. Noah was learning that bullies could be handled by standing right up to them; they are often confused and unsure under their tough exterior.

Dorcas, having seen that Noah had faced off Seymour, came over to him smiling and glad to see him.

"Don't pay any attention to that musclehead Seymour," she said shyly. "He thinks that he is my special friend, but I don't really have anything to say to him and honestly, I find him kind of boring most of the time when he brags about himself or tells me how he beat up on some kindergarten mice."

This was music to Noah's ears, as he felt more deeply about Dorcas than he had let on, even to himself. He now gathered the nerve to say, "Dorcas, do you think that you could get away and come with me tomorrow? I have a perfect place for a picnic and I really want to show it to you."

Dorcas smiled up at Noah making him feel very big and important indeed. "Well," she replied after a slight pause, "I really would like to, but I'll have to get my father's permission first. He wants to know my every move. I don't think I'll ever be able to grow up and make my own decisions. Anyway, if he says I may, I'll meet you by the loft ladder at noon tomorrow. Will that be alright?"

Noah was so pleased with her response, "Whatever you say will be fine with me, I'll be waiting there . . . see you then."

Just then, Madame Total marched over to see what was keeping Orcas from paying attention to whatever it was that she was teaching that day. She, too, had learned to respect Noah, but she didn't really like him to hang around during school time, as she felt that he was a distraction.

"Well, hello Noah, I hope you aren't keeping Orcas from her studies."

"Oh no," replied Noah. "Anyway I must be off." And with that he hurried home as quickly as he could, before Madame Total tried to get him to return to school.

The next day at noon sharp, Noah was at the ladder to meet Orcas and soon enough she appeared.

"I told my father that I was going on a field trip and I didn't say who with. He only said, 'It seems to me that Madame Total takes you on a lot of field trips. Doesn't she ever spend any time in the classroom'? I just smiled and left quickly before he had time to change his mind."

With that the two young mice set off for Lillypad Pond. Their spirits were high, as are the spirits of any who are young, who are going to spend a day out of doors picnicking and having fun.

"I want to introduce you to my new friend Giles, well, he isn't my exactly what you would call a friend, but he is really interesting and can do wonderful tricks in the water."

"In the water!" laughed Dorcas, "what kind of animal is he?"

"He is an otter and they spend most of their lives in and around water," replied Noah. "They eat fish and can dive, swim, turn summersaults and do all kinds of wonderful things."

"Sounds really great," replied Dorcas and the two continued along tiny paths known only to small animals that led them through grass and underbrush, out of sight from circling hawks or eagles.

Soon they could hear the pleasant murmur of Sparkling Stream and over that, the sound of a waterfall, as the stream flowed its way over the small dam that Farmer Boaz had built to create the pond that was home to otters, fish and lillypads plus another animal that Noah had not as yet met but soon would in ways that were not the most pleasant. Now the two mice were at the drying rock and were waiting for Giles, the otter, to appear, and appear he did in a rush of water! He flipped himself out of the pond and onto the rock in one continuous movement. Dorcas and Noah were soaked and coughed and spluttered in confusion.

Giles laughed gleefully and said, "Surprised you didn't I pretty good aren't I?"

"Well, yes," spluttrered Noah, "you might have warned us that you were coming."

"What and spoil the surprise and who is this your girlfriend how do you do?"

Noah was stiff with embarrassment but, after shaking as much water off his fur as he could and trying to help Dorcas dry herself off, he gathered what dignity he had left and said, "This is my friend Dorcas."

"How do you Dorcas? The otter replied, "Have you ever dived or swum in water I tell you there is no other life."

"No, I haven't," a somewhat cool Dorcas said, "and I really think I can wait until I do."

Giles seemed to realize that he was being rude, so he quickly changed the subject. "What would you like to do today if we can't dive or swim how about I take you to some floating lily pads out in the middle of the pond from there you get a wonderful view of the entire area it is really beautiful and it is so wonderful to be able to just float as if you were on a cloud."

Noah looked doubtful but Orcas to his surprise, "why yes, that sounds perfect, but how do we get out onto a lily pad in the middle of the pond?"

"That's no problem," returned Giles, "if you will trust me I'll take you one by one on my back and ferry you to the pads."

"Well, you have to promise no tricks," warned Noah. "No diving or flipping us off into the water."

"Oh never, never," reassured the otter who by this time had quite made up his mind to befriend these two who seemed, as if they would be fun to know. His sharp eyes caught the flash of a fin in the water beneath him and he was off and down into the pond as quick as a wink.

While he was gone, Noah tried to explain the otter's behavior to Dorcas. "It's just the way he is," he said. "I don't think he means to be rude, it's just that I don't think he is used to being with other folk. Do you really want to take up his invitation?"

"Yes, I think it would be fun and I agree with you, I think he is really nice in spite of himself."

At that point, Giles rose up out of the water much more carefully than before, so that he didn't splash either of his two guests. "Who is on first?" he asked, swimming alongside the rock, so that the mice could hop onto his back.

"I'll go first," volunteered Noah, thinking to himself that if there were any danger, it would be better if he knew about it, before allowing Dorcas to make the journey. Noah hopped onto Giles' sleek back and almost slipped into the water, so slippery was the fur surface.

"Hang onto my ears!" called Giles and, as Noah grasped hold of first one then the other of the otter's tiny ears, Giles began to swim very slowly and carefully out to the middle of the pond, where a whole raft of lily pads floated green against the blue of the water. In amongst the pads was the occasional lily blossom, bright yellow or white, these splashes of vibrant color made the pond look like a painting that hangs in a gallery. Giles swam alongside a large pad and Noah hopped off, waving to Dorcas that this was quite alright. Giles swam back for Dorcas and soon she was joined with Noah, the two out in the middle of the pond, but still reasonably safe from enemy eyes because of the overhanging willow tree branches.

The two settled down to enjoy their picnic lunch and were joined by Giles who brought a freshly caught fish to chew on.

"Are you going to tell a story?" asked Giles. "You did promise that you would."

And so, Noah began a story about far off places that he read about. The afternoon wore on and the floating lilly pad became a haven of peace and contentment, floating as it did in the middle of the pond gave such a wonderful sense of being in the world but not of it.

While this perfect afternoon was unfolding, other, darker agents were planning vile and unpleasant things for our two young mice. Seymour, in a fit of jealous rage, had followed Noah and Dorcas all the way from the barn to Lily pad Pond. Seymour did not see the peaceful, beautiful scene. Seymour did not see the blue water, green leaves, the smiling sun. Seymour only saw two young mice having a wonderful time and so, he decided then and there to do what he could to spoil their fun. He had never liked Noah, he thought he was a show-off and a know-it-all, and he could read and speak human talk! What kind of normal mouse could do that? As for Orcas, well, she would be better off with a real mouse, one like him who was strong and could beat up on others who got in the way.

While Seymour was mulling over these dark thoughts and trying to decide how best to ruin the picnic that so angered him he became aware of a small animal regarding him curiously from within some water weeds lining the shore. "What are you looking at, rat face?" he snarled at the strange animal who, upon close examination, proved to be a water rat, a small rodent living, like the otter, in and around streams and ponds. These animals had adapted themselves to a different environment than the barn or farm and had learned to swim and dive and eat different food than their dry land cousins.

"What are you doing here in my territory?" snarled back the water rat whose name was Walter and who could be every bit as nasty as Seymour and was quite prepared to defend his space against any intruder.

Seymour had the sense to recognize that here had met someone his equal in viciousness and altered his tone to one of false friendliness. "I'm just watching those two, they make me sick!"

Walter crouched up on his hind legs to get a better look. "Oh those two, yeah, they are a little much, aren't they? I've been watching them and that silly ass Giles for the past hour. Don't they ever get tired of telling stories and laughing? What's to laugh about I'd like to know, seems I've got enough to do just to keep alive. That foolish show-off, Giles, is always diving and splashing about, scaring off any food I can catch. I'd like to see the last of him!"

Seymour, who was as crafty as he was as bitter and mean, saw that here, in the miserable water rat, he could have a co-conspirator.

"Well," he said, "if we work together, maybe we can get rid of the two mice and then figure out what to do about the otter later."

Seymour had no intention of having anything to do with the otter who was much bigger and more powerful than Seymour. Like bullies everywhere, Seymour would never pick a fight he thought that he might lose. "Let's plan on doing the mice first, so we can plan for the otter later."

Walter, the rat, eyed Seymour suspiciously. "And just what's in it for you, Mouse?"

"Well," hesitated Seymour, not wishing to tell the rat that he had no real reason beyond plain jealousy for wishing harm upon the innocent two, "they have done things to me and my family and now it's time for revenge," he lied.

"Well, revenge can be sweet," returned Walter with a nasty laugh, "so I will help you if you promise to help me with the otter."

"Yes, certainly," said Seymour eagerly, "do you have a plan?"

"I do," muttered the rat between clenched teeth, "and here is what you will do: get over to the other side of the pond and create some sort of disturbance to distract the otter and to get him to leave the lily pads where they are floating. While he is busy finding out what you are all about and if you are good to eat, I will swim beneath where the pads grow and bite through the stem that holds the pad in place."

"What then?" inquired the now trembling Seymour, who did not like the idea that he might be tempting bait for a hungry otter. He did not know that otters do not have mice on their menu.

"What then, you dull witted mouse?" sneered Walter, who, like all water animals, had little use or patience with dry land animals.

"What then?" he repeated.

"Well then, the pad will float free, the two mice will be helpless and the current of water will float the pad toward the dam, where it float over the edge and 'Goodbye little mice'! And neat don't you think? Then we can deal with my problem, the otter."

Seymour, although he intensely disliked Noah and was jealous of the friendship between the two mice, certainly did not wish for anything so final, so brutal, as a drowning. Even his cold little heart could understand the loss that this would be for Dorcas' parents and for Grandpa Ezekiel. To admit fear now, however, would brand him a coward in front of this determined animal who obviously had no feelings of guilt or pity.

"Alright, I'll do it, but that otter better not want me for his supper. Just go and do as I told you and be quick about it, before they decide to come back to the shore."

Seymour scurried across the small bridge that was across the dam and onto the other side. There he crept stealthily to a place in amongst the pond weeds lining the shore opposite the lily pads, where the three were laughing and enjoying just being alive. He began to make a weird sound; it sounded like someone in a great deal of pain. The three picnickers looked up and around to see where and what the trouble was.

"I'll go and see what's up," said Giles. "I can swim over and be back in a second."

"Whatever it is, it sure sounds as if it were in trouble," said Noah. "Can we do anything?"

"No, don't worry yourself," replied Giles. "It's probably nothing. We often hear strange noises out here and it turns out to be just a bird or some animal calling its mother."

Off Giles went, flipping himself into the water effortlessly, his sleek back and tail disappearing beneath the blue of the surface of the pond. As this was going on, Walter had dived deep below the surface, found the stem of the pad that Noah & Dorcas were on and, with his very sharp little teeth, rapidly began to chew through the slender stem. Very soon, and before he ran out breath, Walter had severed the stem and the lily pad began to float free, moving ever so slowly with the gentle current toward the fall over the dam.

Noah and Dorcas did not notice that they were floating free, they were so intent on the beauty of nature around them, that they didn't see the edge of the dam coming closer and closer. Finally, the sound of falling water alerted Noah and he looked up to see that they were heading straight for the dam and would spill over it and be drowned, if he didn't act quickly. But what to do? For once, Noah's abilities seemed to fail him and, as Dorcas began to cry softly he looked about him in helpless desperation. He called out for Giles to help, but the otter seemed to be taking longer to respond than usual.

While this was going on, Walter and Seymour were having a very loud argument out in the open, not caring who heard them.

"You lied to me," snarled Walter. "You said that if I took care of the two lovebirds, you would take care of Giles. Well, I did my share, now what about yours, well, well?"

"I didn't know that you meant that I was to kill him. I'm not a murderer. I don't know how to do things like that. I just wanted to scare them, that's all, not try to finish them off!"

By now, Seymour was in tears. Like most bullies, he was really a coward at heart and could be easily persuaded to back off. Now, however, he had become involved with a water rat, who would stop at nothing to achieve his ends. Seymour was in over his head and he didn't know now which way to turn.

"I have a good mind to push you into the water and let you drown," rasped Walter, as he moved threateningly towards Seymour who, tremblingly, inched backwards towards the bridge.

"Please Mr. Water Rat, don't hurt me," sniveled Seymour backing still further and further until he teetered at the very edge.

"I hate all of you land rodents!" rasped out Walter, ridding himself of all the buried anger that he had always felt at thinking himself second best; not as sleek as the otters, not as fast on land as his barn relations. "I'll show you about double crossing me. I may be just a rat in your eyes, but I've got my pride."

At this moment, several things all happened at once: as Seymour was backed up so far toward the edge of the bridge, he lost his footing, fell backwards with a cry and landed onto the lily pad that was carrying the helpless Noah and Dorcas over the dam and don the waterfall into the swirling whirlpool below. Down the three went and, although the force of the water might not be considered to be much, to three very small mice, it would seem like a torrent. One by one, three tiny heads bobbed to the surface and from up above came the nasty laugh of a triumphant Walter, the water rat.

"That will serve all three of you right and maybe, teach Mr. High-and—Mighty Giles, the otter, not to be so smart and make friends with those not of his own kind." He laughed some more, a high whining sound that reached the ears of a very bewildered otter. Giles who, after venturing off to find the reason for the odd disturbance and finding nothing, had returned to where he thought the lily pad with the two mice was, only to find that it had disappeared. He was searching frantically around, when he heard Walter's nasty triumphant laugh and he immediately dived to swim as fast as he could to the dam. Crawling up onto the bridge, he instantly saw the problem and without a moment's hesitation he dived off the other side and resurfaced beside the struggling Dorcas, who was about to go under for the last time. Seizing her firmly in his mouth, he swam to shore, where he deposited her under the fronds of some water ferns. She lay there, a bedraggled scrap of soaked mouse fur while Giles re-dived and sped back to find Noah.

Bravely struggling to keep his head above water, Giles grasped him firmly in his mouth and swam to where Dorcas was now coughing and trying to regain her feet. Giles laid Noah down gently beside her and said in a very soft voice, quite unlike his usual brash way, "What can I do? Oh my this is all my fault I should have never have brought you land mice out into the middle of the pond I am so sorry what can I do?"

Noah, who now realized what had happened, spoke with a faint voice asking, "Where is Seymour? I saw him fall onto the lily pad as went over. Is he here? Is he alright?"

"Why care about that could for nothing?" Giles wanted to know. "I think he is the one who caused all of this trouble."

Noah had now got onto all four feet and was starting off toward the dam. "We can't leave him," he whispered. "We have to see if he is okay."

"Well you are a finer animal than I am," grumbled Giles. "Wait right here and I'll go back and see if I can find his sorry hide."

With that, he was off, leaving the two nearly drowned mice to dry themselves off and to try to clear their lungs of water that they had swallowed.

When Giles returned to the pool below the dam, he could see nothing of Seymour although he looked high and low.

"Looking for your little barn friend?" hissed Walter from the safety of some reeds lining the shore.

"You! I might have known that you would have some part in this you should be ashamed now where is that other mouse? Get me to him quickly or you will pay dearly."

"He's over there," sneered Walter. "He's more dead than alive I can tell you," and with that, he plunged into the water and disappeared leaving just a faint trace of bubbles behind.

Giles was torn between rescuing Seymour and chasing after Walter to give him a piece of his mind. He decided in favor of Seymour as he remembered that this had really all come about because of him. Giles searched the vegetation lining the pond below the dam and finally, he heard a faint squeak of distress coming from behind a log that had fallen a long time ago and was half buried in the mud.

The otter saw the mouse stretched out as though dead and moved quickly to him, took him up in his mouth and made his way back by land along the shore to get to where he had left Noah and Dorcas. When he returned to the spot, he found that they were mostly all recovered from their near drowning and were anxiously waiting to hear news of Seymour.

"Is he still alive?" asked Dorcas with concern.

"I think so," said Noah bending over the limp body of the once tough and proud mouse, who had caused him so much pain.

"How can you be so concerned over someone who has tried to kill you?" asked Giles.

"I don't like Seymour and I don't really care what happens to him, but I don't want him dead," replied Noah.

He placed both of his front paws on Seymour, rolled him on his back and proceeded to try to pump some air into the mouse's water-filled lungs. After a short while, as Dorcas looked anxiously on, Noah could feel a slight movement beneath his pumping paws.

"I think he is coming around," he said.

Seymour choked, threw up some water and slowly opened his eyes. "What are you doing to me, nimwit?" he spluttered and without any further ado, he got to his feet and staggered off as fast as he could, coughing and spitting all the while.

"He'll be just fine," said Noah. "I guess even a near-death experience like that won't ever change Seymour."

"We had better be getting back," said Dorcas, as she noticed that the sun was further along in the sky. "My father will be getting nervous, if I don't get home soon."

"Yes, "answered Noah. "We thank you for the day, Giles, and we will be back again, but next time, I think we'll stay on shore, as all land mice should do.

"Good bye," said Giles, "Take care come back and tell me some more stories soon I'll see to that miserable Walter Water Rat just see if I don't so that when you come you'll be sure of being safe."

With that, the two slightly damp mice set off for their barn loft home, waving to Giles until he disappeared from view. No one noticed the sneering face of Walter who had crept up to the ferns and was listening very carefully to what was being said.

"We shall see about next time," he muttered, as he hunched his way the muddy bank and into the water leaving Lilly Pad Pond quiet and serene. Only a slight breeze and the bending willow branches once more swept the tranquil surface.

CHAPTER TWELVE

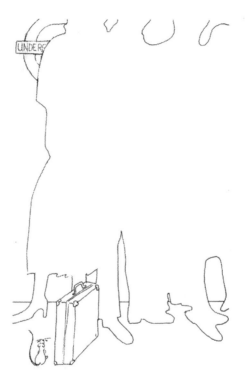

Going Underground

FARMER BOAZ WAS A genial, thoughtful man who tended his farm with love and care. Not for Farmer Boaz the poison or traps for wild animals. His attitude was that there should be a home with enough food for everyone. He didn't begrudge the small amount of lettuce that the rabbits ate or the tiny bits of grain that the mice helped themselves to.

Farmer Boaz was a man of habit and it was his to take off his jacket after lunch each day and nap for an hour or so before continuing his farm work. Our friend Noah, ever observant, noticed this while watching from the barn loft windows. Noah decided that the pocket of this jacket would make a very snug and safe place for him. He could go there to steal away from the sharp, disapproving eyes of Madame Topal and his classmates. As we have said, Farmer Boaz was a man of habit and he always hung his jacket up on a peg placed halfway up a thick wooden pole that acted as a support for the barn.

It was easy for Noah to scamper up the wooden pole, jump onto the blue wool of the jacket and into a snug side pocket that always smelled sweetly of the peppermint candies that Farmer Boaz liked. There Noah would nestle, napping or daydreaming about the things he had read about that morning on his daily visit to the rubbish dump to read yesterday's newspaper.

On this particular day, Noah was curled up inside the jacket pocket snoozing comfortably. He had sucked on a tiny chip of peppermint candy and he felt good and lazy. He had been reading about a city called London. This city really captured his imagination as it seemed to be a wonderful place of fun and adventure. He fell asleep, dreaming of what it would be like to be part of this strange world of people, buildings and cars. Usually, Noah could tell how long Farmer Boaz would take to have his afternoon nap and he would make sure that he was out of the pocket and on his way before Farmer Boaz reached for his jacket. Today was different. The sun had disappeared behind a cloud and a sudden chill in the air woke the farmer from his nap rather earlier than usual. He knew that he had to hurry that day to finish forking up the hay into the loft to store for the winter. He reached for his jacket and quickly shrugged it on, as he went outside to continue pitching hay. After several forkfuls of hay had been pitched up to the loft he was interrupted by his wife who came running to the barn in great excitement. She could hardly get her words out; she was so upset with crying and wringing her hands.

She was upset because their son Dan, who was attending school in the city, had been involved in an accident. A car had hit him while he was bicycling to class that morning and while he was mostly just bruised, his mother felt that her husband should leave immediately for London to see for himself. While all of this activity was taking place, young Noah had been trapped, tossed and turned about. He had to cling precariously to the inside of the jacket pocket. Fear and excitement gripped him just like back to that wild ride the night of the storm made him keen for adventure especially one mixed with a dash of danger. Noah climbed up the inside of the pocket, pushed up the flap with his tiny head and peered out to see what was going on. Everything was a blur as Farmer Boaz bicycled his way to the train station, caught the next train into the city, and there took the subway to Holborne underground station where he needed to get off, as it was near to the hospital where his son was. When the farmer finally came to a complete stop, Noah who had been jiggled and juggled about crawled to the top of the pocket again and lifted the flap. All he could see was a great gaping tunnel that seemed to stretch far off into the dim distance. He could see, running through the center of the tunnel two gleaming tracks of steel from which bounced the reflection of the great glaring lights overhead. He had no idea that this was one of London's busiest subway stations and before he had time to think about where he was, he found himself rudely bounced out of his secure pocket and onto the floor of the platform. Farmer Boaz had reached into his pocket for a mint and, in doing so, had dislodged tiny Noah from his perch at the pocket flap.

"Here then, what's this? A tiny mouse in my pocket!" exclaimed the farmer who stooped to try and pick up the frightened mouse but Noah, confused, took off abruptly, darting helter skelter, madly dodging in and out of the feet of the hurrying crowd of people. The train arrived and with all the noise and confusion, the farmer lost sight of the tiny scrap of mouse. He was swept toward the waiting train by a tide of impatient city folk who only understood clocks, timetables and deadlines. Poor Noah, almost crushed into a pulp beneath the trampling feet, had only one thought: to avoid being stomped upon. Finally, just as all of his reserves of strength were about to give out, he found himself clinging to the edge of the platform by his tiny front feet, a canyon of gravel and tracks lay beneath him. One can only imagine what must have gone through Noah's mind. The clashing of brakes, the thunder of the train, hordes of people pushing back and forth overhead and the smell of rubber, smoke and humans in his tiny nostrils was overpowering to one not used to it. The train left and Noah could cling onto the platform edge no longer, so he let himself fall, landing on a gravelled surface beside the tubes of steel. These looked to Noah like bulging metal muscles. Here, after catching his breath, he burrowed into the gravel and stayed very small and very frightened.

Train after train arrived and departed all day just inches from our Noah. Each time a train roared in he squeezed his eyes shut, clenched his tiny paws and held himself like this until the train departed. The trains themselves, with their lighted windows and sleek cars were so huge, that Noah could barely take them in with his tiny eyes.

For many long hours he stayed rooted to his tiny resting place, not daring to move or hardly even breathe but finally, the last train of the evening pulled out and the station was left in semi-darkness and empty, or so Noah thought.

Rustling noises caught his attention and out from under the wooden planks that the steel rails rested on scurried a whole flock of the oddest looking mice Noah had ever seen and he drew sharply back into his hiding place as he watched them. Without any hesitation or fear whatsoever, they scattered all over the track area. They were chattering to each other in a Nature-Natter that Noah could barely understand, so different was it from the slower speech he was used to on the farm. Noah could make out some words and he gathered that these mice lived here and were on the hunt for food.

Several busily wandered near to Noah, noses and whiskers twitching low to the ground. One, looking up for a moment spotted him huddled pathetically in his tiny hiding hole. With excited chattering, he called out and soon Noah was surrounded by a group of very inquisitive black mice.

These mice were much smaller than the barn and field mice that Noah knew and the thing that set them apart from any mice he had ever seen, was that they were coal black from tiny snouts to twitching tails; a deep black color. Noah knew better than to let their size and color bother him. He knew that mice were mice whatever their outward appearance and that, no matter what color they were, it didn't affect their inner mouseness.

"Who, what, where?" came the questions so fast, and with such an odd accent of Nature Natter that Noah could barely make out what was being said.

He shivered and shook with fear, fatigue and hunger and finally he spoke up and said, "My name is Noah and I'm from far away. I'm lost and can you please help me?"

Much muttering and discussion took place amongst the dusky mice and finally, one of their number was pushed forth and he spoke to Noah in a slower manner, so that he could be understood.

"My name is Sooty and who are you?" All of the black mice had crowded around Noah pushing and shoving to get a good look at this larger tan and white mouse. Noah could see that they meant him no harm and tried to answer as best he could, but could not be heard through all the buzz of questions being asked of him.

Finally, Sooty held up a tiny paw to silence the group, "Now tell us how you got here and who you are and please, be quick as we don't have a lot of time before morning and the trains start again."

Noah, now a little more relaxed although awfully tired and hungry, related the events that had brought him to the dark, dirty place far beneath the vast city. The black mice listened very carefully, only interrupting now and then to comment on Noah's slow drawl of Nature Natter.

"Now tell me please, where am I and how do you live here so far from nature?"

"Nature!" scoffed Sooty. "We left that behind a long time ago and now we live totally on the leavings of humans. We are told by our elders that we came here long ago after a horrendous battle between mouse armies up above. Our ancestors found shelter here while this tunnel was being built and when it was covered over and trains began arriving, our fore-fathers could not find a way out and so stayed here. They adjusted to their new circumstances and made a life for themselves. We are their descendents; we come out when the trains go to bed, and we nest under the tracks and eat what humans have tossed aside. By the way, are you hungry, have you eaten?"

"No," admitted Noah, "not since this morning on the farm".

"Well, here," said Sooty and with that several mice ran up with large fluffy, white objects with odd jagged edges, each one almost as large as the mouse that carried it.

"What is this?" asked Noah, not wishing to offend the hosts but still rather shy about trying new food that he wasn't used to.

"It's called popcorn," replied Sooty, "and it's very good. We get all sorts down here: half-eaten sandwiches, cake, cookies, half-full drink cartons. We never want for food and we think that the humans allow us to stay here because we clean and tidy up the subway."

Noah was enjoying this new salty treat and, for a while, was so busy chomping on its soft, fluffy-white goodness that he finally remembered his manners and asked, "Do you have any water to drink please?"

"What is that?" laughed Sooty. "We don't often get water down here unless a human accidentally spills some from a bottle, but come here". And he led Noah down the track a way and showed him a carton containing the remains of a sweet drink. Noah tasted it and found it very good and satisfying, although he really felt deep inside that none of this food or drink was really as appetizing as the food he was used to at home. The sugary sweetness of the drinks made him feel a little sick and he swayed a bit from side to side.

"Come with me!" ordered Sooty. "You must be very tired and you can sleep while the trains run and then tonight we can finish our stories".

With that, the bossy but kind Sooty cleared a path through the gathered inquisitive mice.

"Stand aside, coming through!" he ordered. He took Noah into a hole under the tracks and down and down they went, until Sooty entered a small den.

"This is my nest" offered Sooty rather shyly. "You can rest here tonight and tomorrow. Right now, I've got to get back up to the tracks for our evening roundup."

Noah sank in the soft nest murmuring, "Round up, round . . ." and before Sooty could turn around to go back up to the top, Noah was sound asleep as he had never been before. Sooty smiled and said to himself, "I think you will make a good friend", and with that he scurried back up to be with his fellow mice.

The next day passed and Noah remained far below the subway tracks. He was grateful to be safe and alive, but he felt surrounded and enclosed by the tiny nest that belonged to Sooty. Sooty was kindness itself, bringing Noah strange dainties from up above. These were things that Noah had never tasted; crumbles of cake, cookies and candy, but Noah was a wild, country mouse used to nature's food and used to fresh air, open skies with forest and meadow all around. Noah appreciated Sooty's kindness but inwardly, he felt nervous and unsure. Up above, in the tunnel, everything was dark, or if lighted, then by large, glaring lamps. Instead of grass or hay to frolic in there was only oily, evil smelling gravel, concrete and steel. The noise was such that Noah felt he would never get used to it or the crowds of people, the dirt and grime. It was overwhelming to a fastidious little mouse who spent a good part of everyday grooming himself.

Spots of oil that couldn't be removed by constant grooming troubled Noah and he knew that this was part of the city life he had often dreamed of. He decided that it definitely wasn't for him.

The next night, after the trains stopped running for the day, Sooty guided Noah to the surface to take part in the evening "roundup".

"What is it? inquired Noah with some fear, after all, he had been taken abruptly from all he knew and thrust into a whole new way of life and it would take time to adjust even if he had an adventuresome spirit.

"It's wonderful, it's fun and you'll see how much you will enjoy it," returned Sooty. Sooty really liked this newcomer who looked and thought differently and Snooty wanted Noah to stay and he wanted to show Noah all that was best about living in a subway tunnel.

"Here they come now!" shrilled Sooty with excitement. From the grey distant ceiling of the tunnel, dark shapes detached themselves and began to fly back and forth.

"Here they come!" exclaimed Sooty, jumping up and down. "Over here, over here." The brown and black bats were leaving their daytime roost where they had hung upside down in the vaulted ceiling of the subway where all was dark and hidden. They were preparing to fly out and begin their nightime hunt for insects, but before they did this, they would often, if in a good mood, give the tiny black mice rides on their back. Noah could see them swooping low and mice hopping onto their outstretched wings, then onto the backs of these flying mammals. Away they would go, up and down in great swirling arcs and somersaults, the mice shrilling in ecstasy at this wonderful treat. Down came a large black bat, its wings outstretched and its mouth wide open, showing rows of white fanglike teeth. Noah had known many barn bats and knew that between the mice and the bats, there was no danger or hostility. So, with Sooty's urging, he hopped onto the bat's back and held on for dear life. Up they floated as effortlessly as a cloud. Then the bat banked and they flew over the platform and the gleaming rails of the station. Noah could see Sooty, waving, far below and got an idea of what the whole station looked like from the air. The bats seemed to have no trouble finding their way in the dark and after many glides, swoops and arcs the bat brought Noah back down to where Sooty was waiting.

"It's time for us to go," said the bat, and with high-pitched squeaks and whistles, the bats brought back their mouse passengers, deposited them gently on the platform and then, in a haze of black and brown, they flew down through the tunnel. They were heading for an air vent, where they could leave the subway and fill the night sky of the city.

"Wasn't that fun?" asked Sooty hopefully.

"It was, it was . . ." Noah, breathless, had no words to describe the sensation of floating far above. He had been taken into the air once before by a hunting hawk but that experience was nothing like this. At that time he had been terrified and held by cruel claws but now he had sat serenely on the bat's back, as he floated to-and-fro about the station.

"Do you think you will stay then?" asked Sooty but before Noah could answer, something happened that set in motion a chain of events that would change Noah and Sooty's lives forever.

Two hooded men had crept very slowly out from behind a pillar where they had been hiding from the night watchman as he made his rounds. The two men had stayed behind after the last train had departed and the subway police had made their checks to see that all was safe and secure. Somehow these two men had not been noticed as they slipped behind the massive pillars that formed part of the station's structure.

All of the tiny black mice scurried off the platform and down onto the subway tracks when the two men appeared. The mice headed for their tiny tunnels to hide until the two should leave. The subway mice often had things thrown at them by people who couldn't appreciate the public service that the mice performed; they kept the station crumb and clutter free. Sooty and Noah also ran, but when Noah heard one man speak to the other, he stopped to listen.

"C'mon, quickly!" gasped Sooty.

"Just a second," replied Noah, "I'm listening."

"Listening? Listening to what?"

"That's not Nature Natter," replied Noah.

"C'mon, let's go!" repeated Sooty, exasperated.

"I said, listen!" commanded Noah in a tone of voice that Sooty had not heard before.

"Can you understand them?" asked Sooty.

"Yes, I can," answered Noah sharply, "Now hush!" and he crept nearer to the underside of the platform upon which the two men were standing.

"Hey man, right here looks to be the best place".

"Yeah, I think so too," replied the other, their faces so hidden by the hoods they wore, that Noah could not make out what they looked like. He knew, or felt, that something was not quite right. Not much escaped his bright and inquiring little eyes and these men, with their whispered words and furtive movements were up to no good, he felt.

"Just place it down there, under the platform edge, and set the time for 8a.m., when most people will be hurrying to work and won't notice our little gift," sneered the other.

"And then ka-pow they'll all be blown to tiny bits," laughed the first with a grumbly, nasty laugh. Then they'll know who's boss and maybe then they'll listen to us and see our cause."

The two men now leaned over the platform ledge, and with tape, fastened a briefcase to the underside of the platform but very clearly seen, if one were on the subway tracks, as Noah and Sooty were.

"What does it all mean?" whispered Sooty.

"It means that we're in trouble if we don't so something and fast."

The two men finished their work and now the briefcase was suspended just below the platform edge, well hidden from view. The two men stood for a moment, laughed, shook hands and left as silently as they had come.

"How do you know what's going on?" asked Sooty.

"I can't explain it all right now, just trust me, do as I say and maybe we can avoid being blown up."

"Blown up?" snorted Sooty, "What are you talking about?"

"Yes, blown up I said" replied Noah. By now the other little black mice had gathered around to hear what the new mouse was talking about and they chittered among themselves about the strange, outland mouse who could understand human talk. Noah now took charge.

"Alright everyone, you must listen to me and do as I say. You must trust me as I understood those two humans and they have left a bomb to explode tomorrow morning when the subway will be crowded with humans on their way to work. We'll all be blown up, you, your homes and everything so do just as I say please." With that, he leapt up to perch on the briefcase, carefully examining it to see how he could get inside. He knew that he could use his powers of imagination to do this, but he knew it would only confuse his new friends. Although Noah knew very little about bombs, he had read enough in newspapers left on the rubbish heap to know that there were a lot of wires involved. He saw that the case was latched and thought that, if enough tiny mouse paws could push together hard enough, they might just have the strength to push and release the catch.

Noah was afraid of what he might find and if he would know what to do when it was opened. He realized that something must be done and so he called for ten of the strongest young mice. Many little mice answered this call but Sooty, anxious to help his new friend sorted out the ten strongest that he knew. When he was finished, Noah instructed them to push with all their might on the small round button on the briefcase latch. After much scrambling, slipping and falling, kicking and squeaking, the mice arranged themselves along the top of the briefcase, their little paws just reaching the button. They pushed; nothing! They tried again using all of the strength in their tiny bodies. This time the button pushed in and the briefcase flew open sending the mice flying onto the tracks below where they landed unhurt. Noah leapt to the mouth of the now open briefcase and through the dim light of the subway at night, he could see round cylinders packed into the case and a maze of wires twining round and round. He stared at this in wonderment, not knowing what to do next.

"What is it?" asked Sooty, who had now leapt up beside him.

"It's a bomb for sure," replied Noah.

"What's a bomb?" asked Sooty.

"It's something that will explode and send all of us and the humans flying into the air. It won't be a fun ride such as the bats gave us. The walls of the station will collapse, the trains will collide and there will be death and destruction everywhere."

Noah very carefully picked his way down into the interior of the briefcase which glowed inside with tiny red, green and yellow lights that winked on and off.

"Oh," breathed Sooty, speechless at this sight.

A very faint hum radiated from the cylinders and a tick, tick, tick from a clock attached to them. Noah remembered reading about how a bomb squad had dismantled a time bomb that had been smuggled aboard a bus and the article had mentioned untying wires attached to the clock.

Noah moved very carefully around the inside of the briefcase. He tried to follow the path of the wires leading from the ticking clock to the apparatus on the cylinders which would set them off.

With extreme caution, he unwound the soft wires, undoing them from the contact points to which they were attached. Sooty watched all of this with great concern, only leaving Noah's side once to warn all the other mice to stay in their dens until he gave the all-clear.

So wrapped up were Noah and Sooty that they did not hear footsteps that brought the two hooded men back to the place where the briefcase was hidden.

"It's all off," said one.

"Well why weren't we told earlier, before we went to all this trouble?" said the other.

"Because the boss says he's still in negotiations, that's why, and we're to get this damn bomb out of here before it's too late."

"Hey! How come this thing's open?" asked one.

"How should I know, you probably didn't close it properly. Now shut up and let's lift this out of here."

With that, the next thing that Noah and Sooty knew, they were locked into the darkened bomb case and were being transported up and out of the subway station very quickly.

Sooty and Noah were bumped about. This was the second time Noah had been in the wrong place at the wrong time and was being transported against his will.

He and Sooty clung on to each other and when the two men arrived at their apartment, they hurriedly opened the briefcase, turned it upside down and dumped out the bomb apparatus. Noah and Sooty clung to the rough interior with their tiny claws. Into the case were being stuffed shirts, underwear and a lot of literature. The mice could hear the men talking and what Noah heard struck fear into his heart.

"The boss says I've got to catch the 12 o'clock plane and I've got to get rid of this bomb, pack and be prepared for something even bigger coming up. The whole gang is meeting with the Big Boss tonight and plans are being made for an explosion that will really rock the world and put us up as Number One."

"What about the station bomb?" asked the others.

"It's just small stuff," replied the first. "This next one is going to make the world sit up and notice us once and for all."

With that, the briefcase was again snapped shut, our two young mice almost suffocated at the bottom of a pile of laundry. The two mice were now aware of being carried, going up and going down, being sprung from side to side and finally coming to a complete halt. They whispered to one another words of encouragement and Sooty said, "Now I know how you must have felt the day you came to our station."

Noah replied, "Well, at least I'm not alone this time."

Suddenly the briefcase gave a small lurch and the two mice heard an incredibly loud sound of motors racing, then they felt weightlessness as they were lifted from the ground.

In a while the case was opened and a hand reached in to take out several objects, at which point Noah decided to act quickly. He grabbed Sooty's paw and yanked him up and out of the case. They fell, unobserved to the floor, catching their breath. They rested for a moment between a pair of boot-clad legs. Noah, sensing light from above, grabbed Sooty again and climbed up to perch in a small window.

The two mice, who were headed they knew not where, were in a large jumbo jet. Noah could barely see through the wisps of clouds floating by, the fields and forests of his homeland growing smaller and smaller as he was lifted higher and higher to where and to what?